Sorlandet

Sail Training
The message of the tall ships

Sail Training
The message of the
tall ships

John Hamilton

Foreword by Lord Burnham,
Chairman of the
Sail Training Association

Patrick Stephens

First published in 1988

British Library Cataloguing in Publication Data

Hamilton, John
  Sail training.
  1. Sailing   2. Youth—Training of
  I. Title
  797.1'24   HD5715

  ISBN 0-85059-906-7

Patrick Stephens Limited is part of the
Thorsons Publishing Group, Wellingborough,
Northamptonshire NN8 2RQ, England

Printed in Great Britain by Butler and Tanner Limited, Frome, Somerset
10 9 8 7 6 5 4 3 2 1

Dedication

This book is dedicated to the memory of Lieutenant Colonel James Myatt CVO whose strength of personality and whose belief in the ability of young people played such a great part in the formation of many of the sail training organizations mentioned in this book.

That strength and belief provides an inspiration for those of us who were fortunate enough to know him and learn from him and who now try to continue the work in which he so vehemently believed.

Acknowledgement

Most of the photographs in this book were taken by Janka Bielak (see page 98), who has a great depth of knowledge of sail training in its many forms throughout the world. This is due to a combination of circumstances: in part, a deep interest in the subject engendered by the firm conviction that sail training is a tremendous opportunity for young people and a wonderful medium through which to meet each other regardless of national characteristics or religious, cultural or political persuasions; also her ability to speak five languages fluently and understand others more than she will often admit; and, finally, to the fact that she has been one of the crew of a small sail training yacht, a medium-sized schooner and a giant square-rigger on different occasions.

Her knowledge and depth of feeling can be detected in the photographs and I am very grateful indeed to her for allowing me to use them to illustrate my subject.

Contents

Foreword
by Lord Burnham,
Chairman of the Sail Training Association

John Hamilton probably knows more than any other living person about all the many aspects of sail training — from the sailing characteristics of 'clumbungays' to the mental processes of inner-city youth. I am therefore delighted that he has at last written this book giving his thoughts and conclusions on the philosophy and practice of one of the most valuable types of character training available to young people in the modern world.

We are all from time to time in danger of taking ourselves and our objectives too seriously. John does not fall into this trap, but he recognizes that there is more to sail training than taking young people to sea for a weekend and bringing them back, in the words of the late Lord Amory, 'full of fresh air and cocoa'. To learn to live and work together as a team in conditions which are often downright unpleasant is a creditable achievement — and sooner or later a kindly Providence produces a reward in moments of sheer content. We are after all in business to provide memories.

One of the great triumphs of the sail training movement over the past thirty years has been the development of an international 'family' of ships' captains and organizers who share the same ideals and work to bring together young people from all seafaring nations. Anyone who has witnessed a gathering of sail training vessels at the end of a Tall Ships Race, and the subsequent interchange of crews between ships of different nations, sizes and types, will readily appreciate the contribution which the shared experience makes to international understanding.

I have been honoured by John's request to write this foreword, but the book ought really to be dedicated not only to the memory of James Myatt but also to the many supporters of sail training who have helped to keep the vessels solvent and thereby enabled the good work to continue.

Songs and Shanties

I am a great believer in the power of song; a well-chosen song can bind a crew together in time of difficulty, in time of celebration or in time of competition. I firmly believe that the best crews that I have sailed with have been those that have come together at one time or another during a voyage through the medium of a song.

It is for this reason that I have included a song at the start of each chapter. You can find the well-known sea songs and shanties in many books and song sheets; quite a few of the sail training organizations have their own song sheets and these are usually popular with their crews. The songs I have included here are, on the whole, quite unusual ones, sad songs, funny songs, celebratory songs. Whatever their theme, they are among my favourites and I hope that you find at least some of them become your favourites too.

Fiddler's Green

CHORUS
Wrap me up in my oilskins and jumper,
No more on the docks I'll be seen,
Just tell me, old shipmates, I'm making a trip mates,
And I'll see you someday on Fiddler's Green.

As I walked by the dockside one evening so fair,
To view the soft waters and take the salt air,
I heard an old fisherman singing this song:
'Oh take me away boys me time is not long'.

Now Fiddler's Green is a place I've heard tell.
Where the fishermen go if they don't go to hell.
Where the skies are all clear and the dolphins do play
And the cold coast of Greenland is far, far away.

Where the skies are all clear and there's never a gale
And the fish jump on board with one swish of their tail.
Where you lay at your leisure and there's no work to do,
And the skipper's below making tea for the crew.

When you get back to docks and the long trip is through,
There's pubs and there's clubs and there's lassies there too.
Where the girls are all pretty and the beer it is free,
And there's bottles of rum growing from every tree.

Now I don't want to have a halo, not me
Just give me a breeze and a good rollin' sea,
I'll play me old squeeze-box as we sail along,
With the wind in the rigging to sing me a song.

ANON

Chapter 1

What is Sail Training and How Does it Work?

For quite a long time I had felt a book about the whole business of sail training 'coming on', and the thing which finally triggered me was an incident which occurred while I was attending a conference on the subject in America. One of the delegates was explaining his ideas for a new organization which he was aiming to set up on the east coast of the United States to enable young people to get to sea.

'Haven't any of you guys written a book about all this sail training stuff?' he asked the meeting.

Apparently no one had, but I had been thinking about doing so and his question triggered me into action — and this is the result. What I am setting out to do is to give you a guided tour along various paths of sail training, to explain what it is all about and to discuss various different methods that have been and are being tried. I intend to describe some of the systems used, some of the organizations which practise sail training and the pros and cons of various methods. I will illustrate many of them with examples of incidents which have actually happened, and I hope you will find many of these amusing.

If you know very little about sail training you are not alone. Most people have sort of heard vaguely of it, perhaps even know the name of a few of the ships but are not too sure what it is really all about. As an example, I long ago realized that when giving the name of my organization over the telephone I have to say:

'The Sail Training Association — that is S-A-I-L.'

Otherwise I either get through to quite the wrong department or, more usually, the company I am talking to does not want to know. It reminds me of several occasions when I went up to the Clyde to do some recruiting of ships for a sail training race we used to hold up there. I decided to do some telephoning around the likely sort of people who might enter, and in the first instance I would ask to speak to Mr MacSporran in an attempt to get him to enter his yacht *Highland Mist*:

'Who will I say is calling?' would come a charming Scots voice.

'The Sail Training Association,' I would announce clearly and with some pride.

'Och no,' I'd be informed. 'Mr MacSporran's in conference just now.' Clearly this was a situation that was going to last all day.

By the second year I had become a bit wiser and would reply:

'The Sail Training Association, S-A-I-L.'

'I'll just see now . . . Och no, I'm sorry. Mr MacSporran is engaged just now.'

But for my endeavours the third time, I tried:

'Good morning. I wonder if I could speak to Mr MacSporran about *Highland Mist*.'

'Och yes!' came the immediate reply. 'I'll put you straight through.'

What is sail training? To those of us who are involved in its practice, it seems that it is quite a wide field but to the outside world it is a small and fairly highly specialized form of training. Perhaps one could say that in its broadest sense it is a form of adventurous activity for young people, the medium of adventure being a ship sailing at sea and away from the sight of land. Of course it is not only young people who can benefit from the experience of going to sea under sail. It is enjoyable and beneficial to all ages and is in fact one of those activities which people can enjoy to a ripe old age. The older you are at the game, the more crafty you become at saving your energy and being in the right place at the right time. However, it is mostly about young people that I shall be writing, for it is in the formative age between, say, 15 and 20 that it can prove so valuable.

There are basically two types of youngsters who can benefit from sail training, those who are undergoing it as an apprenticeship for a sea-going profession and those who are sailing either on a once-only voyage or on occasional voyages interspersed with their ordinary lives ashore. I shall expand on these two facets at a later stage.

There are many types of craft involved in sail training. They are not necessarily sailing vessels, although for reasons which I shall discuss later sail has many advantages over power in this application. There are giant square-riggers carrying crews in excess of three hundred souls, there are open boats with a crew of two and there are all shapes and sizes of ships in between. Different types of vessel suit different forms of sail training, and I will give my ideas as to which is best for what.

I have said that one group of young people who undergo sail training are those who are embarking on a career at sea, and in many countries future naval officers and ratings, merchant seamen and fishermen spend some time at sea in sailing ships as part of the curriculum at their training establishment. In Britain this is quite rare. The Royal Navy has decided that such specialized training does not justify the time and cost involved and confines its use of sailing yachts to adventure training in the same way that their servicemen

Gorch Fock with admirers.

are encouraged to go mountaineering, skiing or gliding. The British merchant service also confines its sailing activities to the recreational use of a small number of sailing yachts, mostly those operated by the Maritime Colleges.

However, the story is very different in other countries where many navies operate large square-riggers for their naval cadets. The West Germans have the *Gorch Fock*, the Spanish have the *Juan Sebastian de Elcano*, the Portuguese the *Sagres*, to name just three. Then there are countries whose navies operate smaller ships for the same purpose, such as Sweden with the two sister-schooners *Gladan* and *Falken* or the French with another pair of sisters, *Belle Poule* and *Etoile*. Then, too, Merchant Navies have the use of sailing ships in some countries, the Polish Merchant Navy Academy at Gdynia has *Dar Mlodziezy* a proud new ship but with a difficult name for non-Polish speakers to try to get their tongue around! Norway uses *Christian Radich* as part of their education system, but in the main the boys who sail in her will pursue a career at sea. They also have two other square-riggers, *Sorlandet* and *Statsraad Lemkuhl*, but these have a slightly different role in that they take non-professionals, an aspect which will be covered a little later. *Sedov* and *Kruzenshtern*, the two largest sailing ships in commission in the world belong to the USSR and are owned and operated by their fisheries board and used as part of the training of future officers and men in the fishing service.

So far, all the ships I have mentioned have been from Europe, but

Above Twins — *Gladan* and *Falken* of the Swedish navy.

Above right The four-masted Barquentine *Esmaralda* from Chile.

Right *Malcolm Miller* with her twin *Sir Winston Churchill* in the background.

countries throughout the world maintain ships for these different forms of training, for example some nine countries in South America have ships, including *Cuauhtemoc, Esmaralda, Gloria, Guayas, Libertad, Simon Bolivar,* from Mexico, Chile, Panama, Ecuador, Argentina and Venezuela to name just a few. Japan has the *Nippon Maru* and *Kaiwa Maru* and in North America, the United States Coast Guard operates *Eagle* for the benefit of their young officers. This is by no means an exhaustive list of the world's professional training ships, but a random sample to give you an idea of the large number in commission. They are by no means all relics of the last days of the sailing merchant ships either. Some are veterans of the '20s, but many were constructed in the '50s or later, with *Cuauhtemoc* and *Dar Mlodziezy* commissioned in 1982. As this is being written, in 1986, two ships of very similar size and construction to *Dar Mlodziezy* are being built in Poland for the Russians.

All the ships just mentioned are for those who are going to make the sea their career. There is another group of sailing ships for those who will sail perhaps just once or for a limited number of times. Examples of these are the British schooners *Sir Winston Churchill* and *Malcolm Miller,* another pair of sisters, the previously-mentioned Norwegian *Sorlandet,* the Dutch have *Eendracht,* the New Zealanders have *Spirit Of Adventure* and *Spirit Of New Zealand.* There are a great many sailing ships both large and small in most of the countries of the world — including such land-locked nations as Switzerland!

Of course the whole business is far less cut and dried in practice for while some ships have established roles, many others have operated different types of voyages at different times. Funding is always a problem, for these sailing ships cost a great deal of money to maintain and run, and even where the navy of a country is paying for the operation of a ship it is nevertheless a battle with the treasury to agree and keep to a budget. Therefore there are many of the group taking non-professionals which play Robin Hood by sailing off to warmer climes for some voyages and crew their ship with adults, who perhaps pay slightly more than the regular crews of youngsters and who, hopefully, will spend a bit of money at the ship's bar. The revenue from such cruises helps to subsidize the voyage fees of the more usual crews of young people. In other cases, the owner of a private yacht may agree to sail once or twice a year with a crew of young people, perhaps from the cadet section of his yacht club or a local youth organization. There are many variations and I shall discuss most of them in this book.

So who are the 'customers' for this form of training? I have said that predominantly they are youngsters of between 15 and 20 because these are formative years and a time when adventurous activities of this sort can have a dramatic impact on one's progress towards maturity. Perhaps, because of a slant of the language, I have given the impression that I am talking only about boys or young men, but this is certainly not the case as many of the organizations take both sexes,

Aztec Lady — competitor and communications ship.

Two — Six — Heave!

Below The girls are full members of the crew in every respect.

Sorting out the spaghetti.

The spaghetti sorted!

both in crews together or on separate voyages. There have been many and seemingly endless arguments about whether sail training is as good for young ladies as it is for young men, which of them does better and so on. I have come to the conclusion that it benefits both but not necessarily in the same way. There is no doubt that at the age of, say, 17 the average girl is mentally considerably more mature than the average boy of the same age, while because of the comparison in physical strength the girls are at a slight disadvantage when it comes to heaving on ropes, hoisting sails and so on. What happens is that they set their attribute against their disadvantage and, age for age, both groups come out level.

This can be shown by a story often told about girl crews in the STA Schooners. If a group or watch of ten boys is set a task, such as the hoisting of a sail, they will barely listen to what they are being told to do, dash off before the explanation is finished, fall all over themselves and the task and, after a considerable period of muddle, end up with the sail hoisted in a reasonably satisfactory fashion. Ten girls being set the same problem will listen patiently and then walk slowly away and stand in a group. Just as you are about to suggest that they should get on with the task, seven of them will go off to set the sail while the other three come back and enquire what you would like *them* to do! There is absolutely no doubt that most of the girls enjoy their time on board every bit as much as the boys and that they get a great deal out of it, but what they learn may well be different.

Now I would like to examine this age factor. I have said that the range of 15 to 20 is the most usual, but there are many organizations who take people either older or younger. Before dealing with the upper and lower limits I think it is important to realize that the range of ages of the crew must be restricted, because what is fun and reasonable for a sixteen-year-old may well be extremely boring and restricting for a twenty-year-old. An obvious example is the frequency, length and location of shore leave, and the way that instruction is put over to the novice crew. We can all continue to learn at any age, but it has been found that this particular form of training is most useful at the time when characters are being formed or, to put it into figures, up to a maximum age of 25. Many of the large Navy-operated square riggers have an average crew age of 24 because these are cadets undergoing the experience as part of their vocational training.

So in broad outline we have seen who takes part in sail training, and we have established one most important fact that is very often overlooked or ignored. It is that the sail training ships, be they giant square-riggers or rather small yachts, are kept in commission by their owners or operators at great cost in order to provide various types of training, usually for young people. One way of looking at it is to say that, like their predecessors, the ships carry a cargo and a very precious one at that, a cargo of young people. I say that this is often overlooked because many tourist and commercial groups are interested in the ships only for their appearance or for the crowds, and therefore the money, that their presence will generate. I have frequently been asked by public relations firms and by film companies such requests as:

'Could you please arrange for two of the big square-riggers to be anchored off the Houses of Parliament on 5 July, as we are shooting a scene . . .'

Apart from the fact that the furthest upriver a sailing ship can go is to the Pool of London, the training ships cannot just be 'whistled up' at the whim of film-makers and others. They all have busy schedules which they must keep in order to justify the enormous sums of money which it costs to keep them in commission and, in turn, so that they can continue with the programmes on their tight and busy schedules.

I feel I should explain the term 'tall ships' at this stage. It is in some ways an unfortunate term, for how tall is a tall ship? The answer to this is rather similar to that of 'How long is a piece of string?' The phrase 'tall ships' almost certainly comes from John Masefield's famous poem *Sea Fever*:

Sir Winston Churchill ghosting past *Sedov*.

'And all I ask is a tall ship and a star to steer her by'.

I am sure that the poet was thinking of the majestic wind-jammers which sailed the oceans as the cargo carriers of their day. Tall ships is an emotive phrase and was borrowed by writers, broadcasters and journalists to describe almost any kind of sailing ship, both old and new, large and small. Hence the Cutty Sark Tall Ships Races which for many years the Sail Training Association officially called the International Sail Training Races but eventually bowed to the inevitable usage of Tall Ships Races. So the phrase is a general one and in practice there are some quite tiny tall ships!

So now we have had a look at the sail training ships and the reason for their continued use in the modern age of the internal combustion engine of ever increasing efficiency. What benefit does a spell on board give the young man or woman? That is a very difficult question to answer because if one is not careful the reply will sound like a Victorian treatise on 'The Advantages, Disadvantages and Moral Implications of . . . .' The best way to find what the effects of time spent on board are is to monitor the progress of a youngster. I can clearly remember a conversation which I had with one of the adults sailing in the *Sir Winston Churchill*:

'John, you do a large number of voyages in this ship and I see that

Apollo is possibly the smallest of the Cutty Sark Tall Ships racing fleet but that did not stop her from taking part in the 1980 transatlantic race.

your son sails as well. Is there a reason?'

'Oh yes,' he replied. 'You see, we were very worried about my son; he had been determined to join the Army from his childhood and then found he failed the medical examination. He was absolutely thrown and did not know what on earth he was going to do. As a kind of breathing space, we sent him for a fortnight in this ship.'

'Did it help?' I asked.

'Very much so. My wife and I were astonished at what a difference just two weeks could make. He came back a very much happier young man with a clear idea of what he was then going to do. All the aimlessness and lack of direction had been replaced by a sense of purpose. I was so impressed that I decided to sign on for a voyage myself to see what had worked this dramatic change in so short a time, and I've been coming back regularly since — so has he.'

Frequently the question is asked:

'We've been trying to help him to grow up for seventeen years. Do you really think you can achieve anything in two weeks?'

The answer is that sail training can. Perhaps I can illustrate one of the powerful factors used by means of a story. The scene is one of the smaller sail training yachts and the crew have just joined on a Friday evening and are getting ready to turn in to their bunks for the night. They consist of the warden and eight lads from a community home, lads that have been in various kinds of trouble and are temporarily in the care of the local authorities. I looked around the eight of them and said:

'Right, Bill, I want you to be our breakfast chef tomorrow. I'll give you a call at six-thirty and I want you to cook the breakfast, ready for half-past seven.'

I then started to show him where eggs, bacon, bread and so on were stowed.

''Ere, I ain't never cooked nuffink,' he said in some dismay.

I ignored him and continued to point out where the essential items were stowed. He continued to mutter that he was not going to be able to manage. I made sure that they were all settling down then went into the aft cabin which I was sharing with the warden.

'You know, I don't think Bill will be able to manage,' he said. 'At the home we never let them into the kitchens.'

'Well if he doesn't, it'll be just about the first time it's failed,' I said.

We left it at that and soon everyone on board was asleep. In the morning, through the thin partition between our cabin and the galley, I could hear the preparations for breakfast getting under way. There was a great deal of conferring, almost breakfast by committee, but our hero was chairman. I ignored the confusion and at the appointed hour of seven-thirty the warden and I entered the saloon for our

The crew of the Canadian schooner *Bluenose*.

breakfast. There was a proud breakfast chef, table laid reasonably, eggs a bit black but certainly eatable and we all enjoyed a hearty meal.

'Never fort I could of dunnit,' muttered the chef.
'Never thought he could either,' murmured the warden.

I never doubted that he would succeed because hundreds just like him had done so in past voyages. One of the great things about life on board is that there is an endless succession of not particularly difficult jobs that have to be done by the crew in order that they and the others on board can survive and function, and that the ship can get to where it is going. These are not contrived but can clearly be seen to be necessary for the well-being of the small community of which each crew member is a part. I suppose it is a 'throw them in at the deep end' policy.

Another story illustrates the need for a group of the crew to work together to achieve some nautical operation. On a great many occasions, even on a tiny tall ship, unless the crew works together as a team, the members will not achieve anything at all and may even damage themselves or the equipment of the ship. Therefore in addition to discovering that they can achieve many things which they did not realize they could, they also learn to work together as a team and, what is more, to live together as a team because even in the large ships, the accommodation is very cramped and quite spartan. If one member of the crew is not doing his fair share or generally acting in an antisocial manner, the others will soon point out to him the error of his ways. The half-deck in the STA schooners *Sir Winston Churchill* and *Malcolm Miller* is about 45 ft long by 24 ft wide and when I have to give an introductory talk to a newly-joined young crew, I often ask them to imagine an area of that size marked out on a football pitch and then to imagine how 42 people could possibly live in such a small area — with all their clothes, with their beds and the tables from which they were going to eat their food. I then suggest that one of the vital things they would have to do to make it work is to keep the place tidy and clean. Once again, it is possible to live in such conditions of confined space and has been done in the case of those particular ships for 20 years. In that time there have been a few people who hated every single minute of their time, but alternatively there have been many hundreds who have thoroughly enjoyed it and gone home the better for the chance. There are also lots who have sailed again several times as young leaders in the scheme but more of that later.

The aim of the STA schooners is:

> To provide a challenge and an adventure which will teach young people the benefit of co-operation, tolerance and how to live together with their fellow human beings.

The London Sailing Project's stated aim is:

> To enable young men to learn those attributes of a seaman, namely a sense of responsibility, resourcefulness and teamwork which will help them through the rest of their lives.

The Ocean Youth Club aims are stated more broadly:

> To provide facilities for yachting and boat-sailing at sea and for seasmanship and navigation generally as a recreation or leisure time occupation to improve the conditions of life of youth from all parts of the United Kingdom and Northern Ireland.

> To give young people between the ages of 12 and 24 the opportunity to go to sea offshore under sail.

> To foster the spirit of adventure latent in young people.

> To inculcate a sense of responsibility among young people both for themselves and the community in which they find themselves.

> To develop close links with young people from other countries through the establishment of affiliated organisations with similar aims.

They go on to say:

> The Club is run on the basis that members pay and work. Those who sail with the Club are partners in an enterprise rather than beneficiaries under a Charity.

I could quote the aims of a great many others of the sail training

organizations, but all have the same theme and are in business to achieve the same for the youngsters who sail with them. If you were to talk to the parents or the employers of those who have sailed with the different organizations, you would discover that in the majority of cases they have been successful. If you talk to the young people themselves, in many cases you will get the same answer, although a fairly standard and rueful reply is:

'I wouldn't have missed it for the world — but I wouldn't do it again for the world!'

Not really true in the majority of cases, for as I have said many of the organizations rely on youngsters who come back for another voyage to help to lead the first-timers.

One thing is certain, life on board is not easy. To the novice seaman just the amount of time spent on deck and in the very fresh air can be tiring. Add to that the fact that the ship is constantly moving in three directions, pitching, rolling and yawing — that alone soon seeks out and tires seldom-used muscles. Now superimpose the work that has to be done day and night, for ships have to be worked 24 hours a day whether at sea or in harbour, and it can be seen that fatigue could easily set in — and often does. Perhaps I have over-emphasized the amount of duty that each member of the crew has to undertake. In practice, those who organize the routine of the ship know full well that they are dealing with young people and, for

Rough weather for young sailors.

The young crew of the smaller training ships often have a tough time compared with those on the bigger ships.

example, there is nearly always a three-watch system rather than the more usual two-watch routine, which means that our hero will, in theory anyway, only be on duty for eight out of 24 hours. Having said that, the periods of duty will be at four-hourly intervals and this also leads to a feeling of sleep loss, and it does not seem to impress the youngsters much when they are told:

'Ah, but you're getting much more sleep here than you would ashore.'

In many cases you can liken the effect of one or two weeks spent in a training ship to that of National Service. Very few people who had to serve temporarily in the services could say that they had enjoyed every minute of it at the time, but in retrospect most men who did their two years will admit that it did them a great deal of good and there are many people who feel quite strongly that it should be reintroduced. It is extremely difficult to summarize precisely what the effect on the crews is, suffice it to say that in over 70 per cent of cases, the effect is that of helping in a large way the process of maturity in the teenager.

I do not for one moment believe that sail training is the only activity that can work these spells. It is one of a number of adventurous activities, all of which have similar effects to a greater or lesser degree, including windsurfing, scuba-diving and canoeing on the water, mountaineering, hill walking, pot-holing or caving and orienteering on land, and gliding in the air. All have that extra 'zing' that comes from the fact that there is an element of danger present. However, most of the activities I have mentioned tend to be undertaken by a youngster in an individual capacity, whereas, as we have discovered, on board ship group tasks are the rule rather than the exception. I have introduced the word danger and I have done so on purpose, because I believe that it is one of the ingredients which helps to produce this effect on those taking part which is so difficult to define. Is it right to expose young people to danger? I believe that the answer is yes, providing certain rules are followed implicitly.

Every adventurous activity has a set of inviolate rules which have been drawn up by the pioneers of the activity and are taught to the leaders and instructors. In virtually every case there are grades of

Dar Mlodziezy at Bermuda.

Lay aloft and stow!

Working their way out on
the footropes . . .

. . . to start putting a stow
on the squaresails.

certification which leaders are bound to hold before they are allowed
to involve, lead and instruct novices. Provided the rules are known
and practised, then the danger is minimized if not removed as a
factor. It is only when rules are broken that the element of danger
causes injury or loss of life, and more than that, it usually takes
several rules to be broken because accidents, particularly at sea, are
the result of a chain of incidents which form over a period of time. I
well remember the sudden realization that such a chain was forming
link by link, incident by incident, while I was in charge of a large sail
training yacht with 12 novice crew and five older people with varying
degrees of experience.

We had sailed from Cherbourg and were on a very short passage to
Bray Harbour in Alderney; settled weather with a perfect southerly
wind allowing us to slip along the Cherbourg Peninsular, greatly
improving our characters. We came clear of the shelter of the land at
Cap de la Hague and had to cross the mouth of the Alderney Race.
No problem, because it was slack water and the tide, which runs
extremely strongly at this point, had not yet started to set to the
south. No problem; not even when someone looked up at the top of
the mainsail and shouted:

'Hey! There's a rip along one of the seams.'
'Right, let's get the main down quickly,' I ordered.

Some of the duty watch went forward to prepare the sail for
lowering and then to operate the halliard winch, but this was when
the first link formed because it was an old-fashioned winch of the
type where the wire halliard wound on to a drum and the drum had
seized and would not let go of the wire — so the sail could not come
down. Right, no problem; keep the yacht jogging along almost
directly into the wind like a nearly stalling aircraft to spill the wind
out of the sail and allow them time to strip the winch, unwind the
wire and get the sail down, while hoping the split along the seam
would not get any worse. Ah, but another problem; the boy who was
assistant navigator had gone to the stern to read the log, an old-
fashioned type which was operated by a long line trailed over the the
stern with a twirling spinner at the end.

''Ere Skip, the log's disappearin'.' Pause. 'Shall I cut it?'
'NO, DON'T CUT IT!' I shouted.

It was disappearing vertically downwards and twiddling up rapidly.
Experience told me that it had somehow got itself around the yacht's
propeller, almost certainly while we were in the nearly stalled or head
to wind situation. In fact, come to think of it I did remember
noticing that for a short time we had been moving backwards through
the water. The second link came because now we had a sail half up
and half down and did not have the use of the engine. It was then
that I realized that we had been playing around like this for half an
hour and that the tide would have started to run strongly to the south

— link three. Those who know the area of the Channel Islands also know that it is an area infamous for poor visibility — my fourth link. So there we are, blundering around in the fog, being sucked into the Alderney Race without the use of the engine and not able to sail properly!

Right, I had to think how to break the chain. The log-line had wrapped round the propeller, almost certainly while the shaft was revolving in astern; someone must turn the shaft by hand in the ahead direction and pull gently on the log-line at the same time. But nothing, the shaft would not turn. So as a fairly desperate measure, I put the engine into ahead gear, started it and stopped it again immediately. This brought success, as I saw the assistant navigator reeling in armfuls of log-line. A shout from forward by the mast, and I looked at the mainsail which was now responding to the tugging of the duty watch who soon had it down and roughly stowed. I started the engine and crabbed across the tide to the harbour, and as we passed the end of the breakwater we came out of the fog into bright, warm sunshine. No problem, no danger, no chain. But it could have been dangerous and it would not have been any one factor which would have caused the accident, had there been one. Now, in truth, that was not a particularly hazardous occasion, but it does illustrate the chain situation.

You must not think of these crews of youngsters in isolation. I will give a detailed breakdown of the various kinds of ships' companies in a later chapter, but for the moment it is sufficient to realize that in every case, where organizations are complying with the rules, there is always a sufficient number of tried and tested mariners on board who could get the ship under control and sail to a place of safety even if every single one of the young crew has become overwhelmed by tiredness, seasickness or even plain fright. Such experienced hands are not necessarily adults. There may well be youngsters who have sailed in the ship before, proved themselves capable of keeping going under heavy weather conditions and are able to 'hand, reef and steer'. Every sail training ship has a rigid routine which runs throughout the day and night and this ensures that everyone gets their full sleep requirement, that they eat at regular intervals and that everyone does a fair share of the work. In addition there are procedures for routine manoeuvres such as setting sail, handing sail, anchoring, berthing in harbour and so on. There are also procedures for emergencies, should they arise, such as fire or man overboard or abandon ship. These are Board of Trade Sports, the name flippantly given to mustering everyone in their life-jackets and going through the abandon ship drill, then the fire drill and talking through the man overboard drill — which is later simulated once the ship gets underway. However, it may have a flippant name but it is not treated flippantly, believe me. The youngsters are overseen very carefully by their watch seniors and this has the advantage that even in a large ship with numerous crew members, each adult is responsible for only a manageable number of novice crew.

On board the training ships there is a lot of extremely expensive life-saving equipment. It is of paramount importance that every single person on board has a life-jacket of a type approved by the appropriate national authority, fitted with certain straps, a whistle and optionally with a light. Nowadays most of us have seen these beautifully demonstrated by air hostesses. As we expect to remain at sea level throughout most of our voyage, we do not have a need for oxygen masks, but every single person should have a webbing safety-harness, with a stout line attached to it and a special clip. This clip allows the wearer to clip on to a solid part of the ship while on the upper deck in bouncy conditions or when working aloft or outside the ship's safety rails. Life-rafts are hideously expensive but absolutely necessary, and what is more they have to be serviced annually and this is not cheap either. However, they have saved many lives since their inception and all responsibly-run sail training ships will carry them. Also needed are flares for signalling that the ship is in distress, fire extinguishers in sufficient number and sensibly-sited, bilge

Two Russian cadets in
Sedov.

pumps, first aid packs, a proper outfit of tools, the list is a long one but vital. The maritime authorities of all countries have lists of recommended equipment for the various sizes of vessel and it is necessary that the operators of training ships are aware of the recommendations and abide by them.

Yes, sailing can be dangerous, but provided the officers of a ship or, to put it another way, the leaders of the young crews, are aware of the dangers and the ship is equipped as recommended, then the danger should be contained. Statistics can be manipulated to prove all kinds of facts, but the safety record of the many sail training organizations throughout the world is an excellent one. The majority of experienced seamen are cautious people and fond of life themselves! Mums and dads should accept that their sons and daughters are no less safe on board the sail training vessel of a responsible and recognized sail training ship than they are in, for example, the family car, the kitchen at home or at a beach party.

On the whole, all the points that I have discussed so far apply both to the professional cadet undergoing his seatime as part of his professional training, as well as to the youngster who does not intend to take up a sea-going career, but who is sailing for the experience that such a voyage can give. I am now going to consider the number of times a young person may sail. The case of the professional is relatively simple because the time on board is, as we have discovered, likely to be part of the curriculum of a college. The time on board is carefully planned to ensure a good balance of theoretical study and the practical work that can be done at sea. The cadet will almost always have just one chance to be a member of the crew of the vessel in the capacity of crew-member. However, if he shows an aptitude for sailing and particularly if he also makes sailing his hobby or sport, then he may well be appointed back to the ship as a junior instructor at a later stage in his career and later still, may sail again in a senior position, even as captain. In many of the ships, each cadet has a number which applies to him, to his kit locker, to his hammock, in fact to everything of his on board. In the Scandinavian ships and others, he may even be called by his number on formal occasions. A man never forgets that number and more often than not it will act as a trigger to remind him of his time on board, a time that is usually recalled with affection and with pride. Incidentally, I have used he and his in this paragraph, for these professional training ships are normally all-male, but this is not always the case, and in fact I know of some extremely able young ladies who sail in key positions on board, perhaps as 'sergeant' of a Scandinavian square-rigger, or mate or captain.

So a young person whose career is to be at sea will probably only sail once in a sail training ship, but the amateur may well sail again after the initial voyage, particularly if he or she has shown powers of leadership and an ability in one or more of the technicalities of sailing. A limiting factor in many cases is that of finance because most of the organizations have to charge quite high voyage fees, and this may prove a barrier to being able to sail again. A few of the schemes that are well-endowed or well-supported and are able to charge small voyage fees have been able to breed their own officers and even their own captains, from the 'ranks'. Provided that such a scheme does not become too inward-looking and provided that it does not allow bad practices to creep in, then it is an excellent thing. For example a new and perhaps uncertain crew member can be reminded that the captain was in exactly the same situation just twelve years ago as the newcomer now finds himself. I shall describe the promotion system for such leaders at a later stage.

A number of experiments have been carried out to determine the optimum length of time that the young crew-member spends on board and this very much depends on two main factors. Firstly the aim of the course, and secondly the size of the vessel. For the professional cadet, the time spent must depend on the overall programme of the educational establishment and on the amount of instruction that it is intended shall be taught at sea. In the case of the square-riggers the period will vary from a minimum of three months to a maximum of nine. There is an extra factor in this case, that of the voyage which the ship is undertaking. Often the big sailing ships, in addition to acting as training vessels are also playing an ambassadorial role for their countries. There may well be a great gathering of ships in connection with some important national event and the head of state of the owner-nation may have ordered that the ship shall attend. In such a case, if to change the crew would be inconvenient, then the voyage length may well be increased. The advantage here is that because those on board have much to learn the schooling can be adjusted accordingly.

Pop Corn and Chewing Gum *by Jeremy Taylor*

CHORUS
Pop corn, chewing gum, peanuts and bubble-gum,
Ice-cream, candy floss and Esquimo pie,
Ach Daddy how we miss Nigger balls and liquorice,
Pepsi Cola, Ginger beer and Canada Dry.

Ach pleez Daddy won't you take us to the drive-in,
All six, seven of us, eight, nine, ten,
We want to see a flick 'bout Tarzan and the Apeman
And when the show is over, you can take us back again.

Ach pleez Daddy won't you take us down to Durban,
It's only eight hours in the Chevrolet,
There's bags of sea and sand and fun and fish in the aquarium,
What a laager place for a holiday.

Ach pleez Daddy won't you take us to the wrestlin',
We want to see a bloke called Sky High Lee,
When he fights Willie Libenthal there's going to be a murder,
'Cos Willie's goin' to donner that bloody Yankee.

Ach pleez Daddy won't you take us to the funfair,
We want to have a ride on the Bumper cars,
We want to buy some Candy-floss and chew it on the Octopus,
And then we want to take the Rocket Ship to Mars.

Ach pleez Daddy if you don't take us down to Durban,
If you don't take us to Jo'burg life's a heck of a bore,
If you don't take us to the zoo, then what the heck else can we do
But murrar out and donner up the uggies next door!

Ach pleez Daddy . . .

Chapter 2

Developments Since 1960

Before the invention of machinery which could power ships, sail reigned supreme. Vessels of all sizes were propelled by the action of the wind on their sails and sail training was universal among seafarers. There was no need for any specialized ships or instructors because wherever a cargo ship, a navy ship, a fishing boat, a revenue cutter or any other craft was working, there would be juniors watching and learning from their seniors. The deep sea cargo ships carried apprentices, who, like the midshipmen in their naval counterparts, would be part of the crew while at the same time gathering the experience which they would need to pass their professional examinations and become certificated officers. On the lower deck, junior seamen would be understudying the able seamen in order that in time they would get advancement. Sail training for the professional seafarer was as automatic as any other kind of technical or specialized training is today. Furthermore, I doubt very much if there was any kind of sail training for those who were not bent on a career at sea, since there would be little call for the non-professional to go to sea. There was very little private yachting and anyway there were so many opportunities for those who wanted to sail that there would be no need for such a specialization. In the nineteenth and early part of the present century there were some magnificent training ships, both naval and mercantile, for the training of the young professionals and they also acted in a similar way to their modern sisters, as ambassadors and splendid representatives for their countries.

With the era of the steam ship and later the motor ship, and the inevitable decline and virtual disappearance of the sailing ship and the host of other sailing craft, there came an interest from those who wished to sail but were no longer able to do so. In the decade following 1930 there were a number of long voyages and circumnavigations made under sail. One in particular was meant to be the forerunner of what so many organizations are doing today, and that was Alan Villier's voyage in *Joseph Conrad*. Captain Villiers bought the old *Georg Stage*, a Danish training ship for boy seamen, sailed her to Ipswich where she was fitted out for her long voyage and then sailed her round the world with a crew of young men. Sadly he received no financial backing and the experiment cost him a very great deal of his own money, and furthermore the outbreak of hostilities in 1939 turned everyone's mind right away from sail training. However, it did get one boost from the war and that was when Alfred Holt realized that far too many of the young seamen in his shipping company were failing to survive having been shipwrecked. He had a theory that they lacked the will to survive the deprivations encountered in the lifeboats and rafts in which they so suddenly found themselves. He discussed this with Kurt Hahn, the well-known educationalist and founder and headmaster of Gordonstoun. Together they decided to experiment with a form of adventurous training in boats and in the hills, where groups of young people would be thrown on to their own resources in order to encourage in them a will to survive when conditions become difficult. They called this training 'Outward Bound' and it proved to be as successful as they hoped, for the percentage of survivors increased markedly as a result. This Outward Bound training was continued after the war, no longer for merchant seamen but for young people from all walks of life and many occupations. No longer were they being trained to survive the elements, but for survival and improvement in their lives and in their careers. The early Outward Bound courses were closely involved with the sea. At Aberdovey they operated the *Warspite* and at Moray the *Prince Louis*, and both schools also had a number of cutters and other small, open craft which could be either rowed or sailed. Nowadays it has been decided by the movement that the offshore vessels are too expensive to maintain and use up a disproportionate amount of the available funds and therefore they have been sold, and the emphasis put on the use of the canoes and other small craft.

Both before 1939 and after 1945 the uniformed youth movements, in particular the Sea Cadets and the Sea Scouts, had a certain amount of small boat training, but there was very little offshore sailing in yachts or training ships of forty foot and upwards. It was about 15 years after the end of the war that an increased awareness of what this could do to help young people became apparent.

The period between 1958 and 1962 was a most important one for the sail training world for it was during those four years that a great many of the schemes were founded. Perhaps founded is the wrong word because what really happened in most cases was that those involved in small existing organizations decided that the time had come to consolidate what they had been experimenting with, form a recognized club, association or project, and either buy a more suitable boat or increase their existing fleet. I cannot really put my finger on the reason for so many clubs beginning at the same time. Perhaps it was related to the period of time since the end of the war, perhaps to the financial climate of that era because until then we had 'never had it so good'. Perhaps it was that those involved with teaching and training young people realized that the degree of help which they needed outside the formal limits of the classroom was becoming better. At any rate in Britain both the Ocean Youth Club and the London Sailing Project were founded in 1960.

These two sail training schemes did a great deal towards the establishment of further organizations as did the Sail Training Association's International Sail Training Races, as they were then called. The first of these had taken place in a blaze of publicity in 1956 with a race from Torbay to Lisbon. This was the original idea of a London solicitor, Bernard Morgan, who believed that the last of the world's great square-riggers should somehow be brought together and that the best medium for this was probably to organize a race for them. He was not a man of the sea himself but he spoke to a great number of influential people, among them Lord Louis Mountbatten and Captain John Illingworth. The result was that a committee was formed from a number of people who did know about the sea and ships. The Royal Naval College at Dartmouth agreed to host the ships with a magnificent programme of events based on the River Dart, and the Portuguese Ambassador in London, Senhor Pedro Theotonio Pereira, himself a keen yachtsman, backed the enterprise and influenced Lisbon to be the goal for the end of the race, where another grand programme was organized for the crews of the participating ships. Twenty ships from 11 countries took part in this race, the first of its kind for many years — if not the first ever. After it was all over many people felt that it had been such a success that it should be repeated at regular intervals and the Race Committee formed the nucleus of the Sail Training Association, founded in 1956. Their main purpose was to organize an International Sail Training Race every second year and so they did in 1958, 1960 and 1962, all taking place in European waters. In 1964 they very much increased the scope of the races with a series starting at Plymouth to take the fleet again to Lisbon, then from Lisbon a long haul to Bermuda from where the fleet cruised to New York before the European ships sailed back across the North Atlantic to their home waters. This was a round voyage of some 8,000 miles and kept the fleet and its officers together from May to August. Such a long period meant that many friendships were forged and there were many opportunities for enthusiasts from a number of countries to talk about their own sail training scheme and its operation and to swop ideas. This in turn lead to an increased interest in this rediscovered form of training for youngsters.

The Sail Training Association which had been organizing its races now for eight years was a little embarrassed at not having a sailing ship of any reasonable size or prestige to take part in its own events. The Norwegians could, and on occasions did, produce three square-riggers and most of the European maritime countries had entered impressive vessels. Now at about this time, an independent group of people in Britain had been seriously considering building such a ship but were concerned that the funds to build it might not be

James Myatt with crew and friends prior to the start of the 1964 transatlantic race in *Tawau*.

forthcoming. Certainly the government was not directly interested, the Royal Navy had made a decision in the '30s that sail training was not a viable form of training for its officers or ratings and the Merchant Navy did not believe sufficiently strongly to build a ship either. So it was left to the enthusiasm of a group of private individuals to go ahead and build a ship themselves — not an altogether unknown state of affairs in Britain!

It was the 1964 Sail Training Race and, in particular, the efforts of the small British yacht *Tawau* that caught a number of people's imagination. It was announced by the Sail Training Association during its 1962 race that the next race would be a transatlantic event. This fired the imagination of a young Army Officer, Captain James Myatt, who had been involved in sail training in its embryo form since the age of 16 when he had been a very keen Sea Scout. He had helped to organize a crew of Scouts in both the 1960 and 1962 races in *Nordwind* and *St Barbara*. The latter was the flagship of the Royal Artillery Yacht Club and some of the senior members were not too pleased at their pride and joy being sailed, during the high season, by a group of scouts with not the slightest connection with the Royal Artillery.

One very fiery Colonel was particularly outspoken on the subject. However, James invited him to sail in *St Barbara* one weekend when he had planned to take the young race crew on their first session of race training, a fact that he forgot to explain to the Colonel. On the way down to the boat, James asked each youngster to think of three questions such as:

'How do you tie a bowline?'

'What is the Luff of a sail?' and so on.

Once under way, on those occasions when the Colonel was seen to be getting rather explosive and red in the face, an innocent young scout would come up to him and ask if he had time to show him how to tie a bowline, what was meant by the Luff of the sail or whatever.

'Such a nice group of lads,' said the Colonel once he was back at the barracks on the following day, 'and so keen to learn.'

With his imagination fired, James was determined somehow to enter the 1964 race to the States. He had to find a suitable boat, enough money and a reliable and compatible afterguard, that is his other officers, the navigator and watch-keeping mates. This last problem was already solved, for the afterguard on the previous races had 'clicked' and become firm friends. Furthermore they had proved their ability not only as seamen but also as leaders of young people, two attributes that have to be present in equal measure in all who take youngsters to sea. He felt that the finances would be obtainable, but the boat was a problem. In his mind's eye he had the perfect boat for the purpose, but how was he to find it? For 18 months he looked and asked. He and some of his friends combed through the large number of entries in Lloyd's List of Yachts and produced a short list of possibilities. The owners to whom they wrote were considerably surprised at the request to lend their yacht. When nothing seemed to be forthcoming, James announced a cut-off date of 28 February 1964, and that was running things a bit fine because the race was due to start in May that year. Then, while in Mashford's Yard near Plymouth, he saw the yacht that had been in his mind since 1962, a beautiful 52-ton yawl named *Tawau*, built in the early part of the century.

'Who owns *Tawau?*' James asked the yard owner.
'Why, she belongs to Lord and Lady Boyd up at Ince Castle,' was the reply.

James rushed to the telephone box and feverishly dialled the number, four pennies clanked into the box and he was through. He gave his name to a surprised Lord Boyd and it was agreed that he could come up to the castle right away to talk about *Tawau*, so off he set deep into the hinterlands of South Devon and Cornwall. When he arrived, he was shown into the drawing room and a startled Lord Boyd looked at him and said:

'Who did you say you are?'
'James Myatt, Sir,' answered James.
'Oh, I see; I thought you said Miles Wyatt on the telephone.' Miles Wyatt was at the time the Chairman of British United Airways, owner of the yacht *Bloodhound* (later to be owned by the Queen), Admiral of the Ocean Racing Club and a well-known man in sailing and business circles. James Myatt was a young army officer and not very well known, certainly to Lord Boyd.

'Well, now you're here you'd better tell us what all this is about.'

James decided to take the bull by the horns and replied in a rush:

'I saw your yacht, *Tawau*, while I was at Mashford's yard and she is exactly the boat I have been looking for. Could I borrow her to sail across the Atlantic,' and he added 'with a young crew?'

This was rather a startling question from a complete stranger, quite young and slightly wild-looking. However, they discussed the matter in considerably more detail and after thought Lord Boyd said:

'Give me a week, to find out about you and the other adults you have said will be going with you. If I decide to allow this, we can get the whole business fixed up with my agent.'

It seemed like the classic 'Don't call us, we'll call you' situation, but exactly a week later Lord Boyd telephoned James and said that he was prepared to lend the yacht. All Systems Go! There was very little time left before the start of the race, and the crew had to be selected, money raised, stores listed and ordered, modifications made to the boat — a welter of work. But it all got done and *Tawau* with a crew of boys from all over the country, literally from Stornoway to Falmouth, set off from Plymouth to race to Lisbon and then to Bermuda.

It was while we were in Bermuda that an incident occurred which linked the earlier days of sail training with the present time. Whenever a sailing ship is secured to a quay, there is an almost continuous series of on-lookers and after a while those on board become conditioned to being watched and no longer pay much attention. Sometimes, however, one of the spectators will have a different air about him and on this occasion there was just such a man, looking at *Tawau* in a way that somehow showed that he knew about what he was seeing. I was the only person on board because I was on duty for the day, and I asked him whether he would like to come on board and have a look around. He said he would like that very much and on he came. I showed him around and while doing so explained what we had done so far and about the crew of youngsters, whose average age was 17, who had brought us across the Atlantic. He had told me his name when he first came aboard but I had not heard it properly and did not like to ask him to repeat it. However, his interest in our adventure and the sort of questions he was asking prompted me to apologize that I had not hoisted in his name.

'Alan Villiers,' he replied.

What a fool I was! Most readers of this book will know of Alan Villiers's experiences under sail and the marvellous books he wrote, vividly describing those experiences and of his round-the-world voyage in *Joseph Conrad*. Indeed he now said:

'In one way it makes me sad to see what you are doing because it is the same as I was trying to do before the war. I spent a great deal of time and I might say money to try to set up the kind of activities for young people which you have been describing and which are obviously being successfully accomplished in Europe.' Here then was a link between what had happened until 1939 with what was happening in 1964.

When we left Bermuda it was to cruise in company with most of the other ships that had raced with us across the Atlantic to New York. Another exercise was undertaken on this part of our voyage which was to pave the way for a future activity in sail training. James Myatt arranged with the captain of the Norwegian square-rigger *Christian Radich* to take one officer and four lads on board his ship and a similar number would transfer from them to us. I was extremely fortunate to be 'the officer' and so got the chance to sail out of Hamilton Harbour and take a four day passage to New York on board. Inevitably there were many stories arising from this exciting experience. Because of my inability to speak Norwegian, there were not many things I could do on board; for example I could not keep a watch but had to content myself with being on watch with the Chief Mate. However one of the few tasks I could be given was that of operating the ship's radio, for although all the officers spoke extremely good English, some of the American jargon that came over the radio was difficult for them. One morning I was standing by in the radio room when I heard one of the other Norwegian ships calling us:

'*Christian Radich, Christian Radich* this is *Stratsraad Lemkuhl*, kom . . .'

I thought rapidly and then replied:

'*Stratsraad Lemkuhl*, this is *Christian Radich*, I'm sorry but we do not speak Norwegian here. Over . . .'

The air then became full of long streams of puzzled Norwegian and the First Mate, Fred, rushed into the radio room and snatched the microphone away from me.

'What are you doing?' he asked. I was relieved forthwith of my task as unofficial radio operator.

Despite my attempts to help all five of us had a fantastic time sailing in a full-rigged ship with a very friendly group of people who went to great lengths to explain to us what was going on. Once in New York we all rejoined our own ships; we had pioneered something that the Sail Training Association would incorporate into their future races, the Crew Interchange.

After New York, we sailed to Boston and then to Marblehead from where after receiving hospitality that was almost embarrassing in its thoughtfulness and generosity, we sailed back across the Atlantic to Plymouth and a champagne welcome from Lord and Lady Boyd, before we handed back a travel-weary *Tawau*.

'Land's End Radio, this is *Tawau*, I have one telegram, Over . . .' The

Christian Radich and
Kruzenshtern dwarfing the
spectator boats at the
Gothenburg start in 1978.

telegram was to HM The Queen and I had hoped the operator would be impressed. He wasn't and merely asked me for the text:

> The Officers and Young Crew of the Yacht *Tawau* send spirited and loyal greetings on re-entering British territorial waters on completion of the 'Tall Ships' races and Operation Sail 1964 = James Myatt +
> NNNN

Great was our excitement on board, but not from the operator of Land's End Radio when we received a reply:

> Please convey to the officers and young crew of the yacht *Tawau* the sincere thanks of the Queen for their kind and loyal message of greetings, which Her Majesty greatly appreciates =
> Private Secretary +
> NNNN

I have spent some time on that particular voyage because it acted as a catalyst to a number of ideas which had been in existence for some time and caused them to be put into practice. On their return the officers and crew gave a considerable number of lectures to various charitable and other organizations, telling them about what they had done, the experiences they had undergone and what they felt it had done for them. *Tawau* had been the Sail Training

Duet — lent to the Ocean Youth Club by the Reverend Christopher Courtauld.

Association's official entry in its own race because she was British
registered and British crewed and because the STA did not have any
ship of its own, let alone a reasonably-sized one. But there were plans
for a 300-ton schooner, designed by Camper and Nicholson to
replace the Southampton School of Navigation's *Moyana* but put on
the shelf when the school decided to buy *Halcyon* instead. Through
the generosity of the school the plans had been made available to the
STA and now, with the inspiration of the *Tawau* voyage behind them,
building started and culminated in 1966 with the launching of *Sir
Winston Churchill*, a vessel of considerable prestige for Britain and one
which would enable regular voyages with crews of 39 young people to
be made throughout most of the year. This, in turn, gave rise to
another ship, a sister schooner named as a memorial to a son of the
principal benefactor, Sir James Miller — the *Malcolm Miller*.

I have mentioned the Ocean Youth Club which had its origin in an
experiment conducted by an Eton master, Chris Ellis, and his friend
the Reverend Chris Courtauld. These two experienced yachtsmen in
their yachts *Theodora* and *Duet* started to run voyages for public
school boys and children from less privileged groups.

The London Sailing Project had a similarly experimental birth.
The then Minister of Agriculture and Fisheries, Mr (later Viscount)
Heathcote Amory owned a small yacht, *Ailanthus*, which he kept in
the Medway and in which he found himself able to relax from the
rigours of parliamentary duties and public life. His only problem was
that quite often he was only able to plan a sailing weekend at the last
minute and then found that he had not got a crew. A fortunate thing
for him was a meeting with Commander Walter Scott, who was at

the time the Sea Cadet Area Officer for London whilst also running a Sea Scout unit in his spare time. When the Commander discovered Lord Amory's problem he was quick to realize that he was in a position to help and, at the same time, get some exciting offshore sailing for his Scouts and Cadets. To the benefit of both owner and youngsters an arrangement was set up whereby Walter Scott would provide eight lads each weekend and the owner would sail with them if he could get away from his duties. After two years Lord Amory, realizing how much the lads were gaining from their short sailing sessions, decided to set up an experimental project and buy a large yacht so that more London youngsters could sail. He named it the London Sailing Project and bought a 77 ft yacht named *Rona* for which a mooring was found in Portsmouth Harbour. Commander Walter Scott then looked after her and *Ailanthus* which was moved from the Medway to join her. This experiment flourished and I describe its later years in Chapter 3.

So that was something of the period from 1960 to 1964, a most important one for sail training in Britain and there were similar stirrings abroad as well. The Sail Training Association did grand work with their two schooners and what with the 170 adults and 1,100 young crew members that they were introducing to offshore sailing each year together with a similar number accounted for by the Ocean Youth Club and London Sailing Project, a number of other

Hands stowing the sails aloft in Royalist.

organizations were formed to make available similar opportunities. In 1968 the Sea Cadet Corps decided to commission an offshore sailing ship of their own. They gave very careful consideration to its size and rig and eventually built a slightly unusual vessel, *Royalist*, a 90 ft brig which was ready for her first sail training voyage in 1970.

At the same time another experimental sailing project got started, *Captain Scott* owned by the Loch Eil Trust, but sadly this one was not to last for more than five years. Here was a marvellous opportunity for youngsters, for the course in this ship was very much modelled on those of the Outward Bound schools, and in fact you could say that this schooner was a floating and mobile Outward Bound school.

The crew signed on for four weeks and joined the ship at Plockton in Ross-shire or at Loch Eil. These are harbours on the north-west coast of Scotland in a wild and beautiful area which might have been designed especially for sailing and for adventurous activities. So far

Captain Scott setting 13 of her 14 sails.

north was the ship that she reversed the usual custom of yachtsmen who like to tie a sprig of heather under their bowsprit if they have sailed north of Ardnamurchan Point; in the *Scott* the heather was tied there if she came south of the Point! The boys' time on board was divided into a week's sailing, followed by a three-day and two-night expedition into the hills then a further week at sea, followed by the second expedition of two days and one night. There was another week's sailing and then the final expedition of another three days and two nights. Now these shore periods were not just hikes over the moors, they were full-blown expeditions into very wild country in the North of Scotland. For the final expedition, the lads would usually be dropped off at, say, Loch Torridon, and given several points to visit, often places at heights of over 3,000 ft. Meanwhile the ship would be motored by the permanent crew to another loch some 50 miles away, say, Loch Inver where the crew would be picked up. *Captain Scott* was a 480-ton topsail schooner, which crossed fore yard, lower topsail, upper topsail and topgallant yards, plenty for the crew to do aloft, the details of which are covered in Chapter 5. The rig was good in that although it was a fore and aft rig, the design was much more like a square-rigger with no running backstays and with square-sails that could be set even when the ship was sailing close to the wind.

These yards provide a great challenge; working on them, right out at the ends, looks far more dangerous than it really is. I am reminded of three young Borstal boys who were sent to the *Scott* from Glasgow, two brothers and a friend of theirs. They were delivered to the ship in a sort of caged lorry, with a member of the staff to hand them over. They were not happy and scowled down at their feet when talking to anyone. The ship was secured to a large buoy off Plockton and they had only been on board for a very short time before one of them came up to the mate and said, in a very thick Glasgow accent:

'We's's waantin' aff!' which being translated is 'My brother and my friend wish to leave your vessel.' When advised that this was not going to be possible, the reply was:

'We's's waantin tae see the Captain!' Unfortunately the captain was engaged and unable to see them, which they were told. It rapidly became apparent that they intended to jump ship on the following day when she went alongside at Kyle of Lochalsh to replenish with fuel, water and stores. The captain was told of this and arranged to re-supply from the ship's boats rather than going alongside and instructions werre issued for the three Scottish gentlemen not to be in the boats but to be kept busy on board. Quite by chance this took the form of them working aloft doing some maintenance on the square-sails and it was soon seen by the Bosun that they had no fear up there. In fact they loved it and leapt about the rigging like three happy monkeys. This gave the Mate an idea; to make each of them into a yardsman for a particular yard, then before the square-sails could be set, they would have to swarm aloft and let go the holding ropes or gaskets as they are called. The sail could not be set until they shouted down that they were all ready. They were up aloft looking down on the rest of the crew below and it was they who determined when the next stage could start. Well, something changed those three lads. They loved the ship, they started to chatter away to the other lads in the crew, they were able to stand up and sing about 'Three craws sat upon a wall, on a cold and a frosty morning' at the final crew's concert and when the caged lorry and member of staff came to collect them a month later, he could not stop commenting on the change in them. They were standing up straight, looking him directly in the eye and talking non-stop about the ship and its voyage.

'It wis magic, so it was, Sorr. We's no wantin' tae get aff.'

Sailing in such a remote area, yet with many safe harbours and anchorages, makes for some interesting exercises. There was a time when the Captain, Commander Victor Clark, wanted to take the ship into Upper Loch Nevis and this involved navigating through a very narrow and torturous channel from the lower loch. It was decided to send the three watches ashore in the boats being propelled by oars, none of which were fitted with engines, so that each could build two cairns or piles of stones, on pre-determined positions and then paint them white. They then came back on board for a meal, followed by another trip in the boats which they had to line up on their cairns and row in on the line, taking soundings with a lead-line as they went. The following morning the Cpatain piloted the schooner through the narrows using their three sets of leading marks as his guide. A very satisfactory navigational exercise brought to a practical conclusion.

The great remoteness of the Highland coast is unusual in this day and age. On occasions the ship would anchor in a sea loch where there were no lights to be seen and this often meant sending a boat ashore with a paraffin lantern which was set up on a rock and used by the anchor watch, by means of compass bearings, to make sure that the ship was not dragging her anchors. Of course, someone had to remember to collect the lantern again in the morning before the ship sailed and this story may explain a number of rusty and abandoned hurricane lamps dotted around remote rocks in the North West of Scotland. On some occasions, particularly in June, when it hardly got dark, it was not necessary to plant the 'will o' the wisp' and instead the peak of a hill or some similar natural feature could be used to take bearings. This business of leaving two young crew-members on anchor watch, briefing them on how to check that the ship was not dragging, to do a regular patrol to make sure that all was well and that, for example, no fire had broken out or other marine disaster had occurred unnoticed by those asleep, is an extremely important part of enabling them to shoulder responsibility without supervision whilst giving them the option of calling a ship's officer if things appeared to be getting or were actually getting out of control.

'. . . and don't hesitate to call me if you are at all unhappy about any of the things I've told you,' would be the end of a briefing, which led to the unforgettable awakening of the mate one night, to hear a startled and frightened young voice saying:

'Sir! You know that mountain you told us to take bearings on? Well, it's moved round to the other side of the ship!'

The *Captain Scott* course was a splendid one, but sadly it was extremely difficult to finance and so, after only five years of operation, the Loch Eil Trust had to abandon the whole scheme. The ship was subsequently used for one or two similar schemes, but was eventually sold to the Sultan of Oman for the training of young Omani Naval personnel; she is now named *Shebab Oman* (Youth of Oman). Happily the *Royalist* programme, started at the same time, was much more long-lasting and is described in Chapter 3. It was not only in Britain that sail training was getting under way for the youngsters who were not necessarily going to make a career at sea.

The Scout movement has used sail training for some years now as one of its methods of providing adventurous and outdoor activity for its members. It is interesting that the first camp organized by Lord Baden-Powell was on Brownsea Island, in the middle of Poole Harbour. As is the case in formation of virtually all the organizations, it is the powerful personality of one or in some cases a very few people who get things started and so it has been with the Scouts. The birth of offshore sailing in the movement was probably at Marlow where Joe Habens enthused a group of keen young Scouters who, in turn, caught the imagination of some of their Scouts and hence a Scout crew raced *Nordwind* in the 1960 Tall Ships Race. Shortly afterwards a number of yachts started to be used on a regular or semi-regular basis. Ken Wright formed the Colchester Scout Group using *Ramrod* and subsequently two other small offshore yachts and, in London, Michael Nadin and a group of friends took many of the lessons that they had learnt from the London Sailing Project and started the Discovery Sailing Project, originally based on Captain Scott's famous ship of that name and, when she was moved from her berth on the London embankment, they moved ashore to West India Dock and subsequently into a Dutch Pilot Cutter which they bought, re-fitted for their specialized purpose as a headquarters and living ship and named the *Lord Amory* after the founder of the London Sailing Project and long-time Chairman of the London Federation of Boys' Clubs.

Another development of the late '50s was the Island Cruising Club, although their aim is not that of sail training but to provide a fleet of boats of all sizes for their members and thus enable them to sail without the expense and worry of either owning and maintaining their own craft or the great expense of chartering for the times they want to be at sea. Most of them go sailing to increase their experience and inevitably they are learning all the time during their cruises. They have boats varying in size from small dinghies to large

Hoshi — an elegant
Edwardian schooner.

offshore craft and all are maintained and sailed to a very high
standard. Perhaps they will forgive me for calling their operation sail
training without age restrictions.

Of course the learning, the enjoyment and the general benefits do
not have to stop at the age of 19, 21 or 25, and I am reminded of
the adult cruises which many of the organizations run, often at the
beginning and end of the season when the weather around the coasts
of Britain is not as co-operative as in the middle of the year. I am
reminded of one splendid old gentleman who had indubitably
become muddled over his age when applying for the berth for he was
well over 70 — and considerably deaf. However, his keenness was
quite beyond dispute and he 'two-six-heaved' with the best of his
watch, so much so that whenever what was being heaved had to stop
being heaved it was rather difficult to persuade him to stop! However,
his main difficulty was that of steering, which he loved and which
made his eyes shine like a teenager's. His concentration was fierce
and his pride such that he was determined never to be even a degree
off course, with white knuckles his hands gripped the wheel as he
deftly swung it to port and to starboard.

'How's your head?' from the officer of the watch.
No reply. A louder roar: 'HOW'S YOUR HEAD?'
'Do please be quiet, I'm trying to concentrate!'

Resignedly the OOW walked across to the compass to check the
course. The lack of an answer was very little aggravation when

compared to the pleasure that the ancient helmsman was experiencing, that is until it was time to change course.

'Alter course to 120 degrees,' brought another exhortation for quiet from the helmsman. In the end it was found that the only way to change the course without offending the old gentleman was to persuade him away from the wheel for a short while, put on a new and rather more sprightly operator, change course and then hand back the wheel to him again, whereupon he spotted the new course and off we went. When asked why he did not wear his deaf-aid on deck he came back with the understandable reply:

'Ah well, you see, it amplifies the roar of the wind and the sea and makes everything considerably worse; you wouldn't want that, would you?'

In addition to the pure sail training clubs, projects and associations that were formed to provide offshore sailing during the spring, summer and autumn seasons, there grew up a number of other operators of offshore yachts with similar aims, some of which were a water-borne extension of their land-based training schemes, such as the Outward Bound Trust. Several other shore based centres have operated or still do operate small offshore craft, youth clubs, public, state and sailing schools, maritime colleges and so on. Mention of the Outward Bound Trust reminds me of Gordonstoun which operated *Pinta* and then when she became too old, commissioned *Sea Spirit* to enable their boys, and later girls as well, to benefit from a very similar exercise to that carried out by the Outward Bound Trust.

The Armed Services also engage in sail training activities combined with adventure training. At Gosport they have the Joint Services Sailing Centre, started in 1970 with three sizes of craft, 24, 32, and 55 ft to enable the servicemen to start small and build up their confidence, experience and ability as they progress upwards, or to try sailing once and then possibly decide that they are better suited as mountaineers. In addition to the Centre, many establishments such as the Royal Naval College at Dartmouth have offshore craft available for their cadets or, as in the case of the Royal Military Academy at Sandhurst, a yacht club with one or more yachts used for the same purpose. There are also quite a number of craft funded by non-public money owned and operated by Service clubs both for the pleasure of their members and also for use in adventure training exercises.

Then there are a number of private owners of yachts who are prepared to put them at the disposal of the sail training organizations for all or some of the season, either skippered by themselves or lent directly. Such owners frequently enter their craft in the Cutty Sark Tall Ships races, thus widening the chance for youngsters to take part.

Most of these current organizations grew up in a rather random fashion from about 1955 onwards. As I have explained, in each case it was usually due to the foresight and personality of one man. That man was usually fiercely protective about his own scheme, and so no one was surprised that when Lord Dulverton, amongst others, suggested that there was a need to form a national association to represent and protect these fledglings, the suggestion was not met with much enthusiasm. However, in 1970 the Association of Sea Training Organizations (ASTO) was formed and despite their worst fears, it does not seem to have done them too much harm; it has not tried to do their job for them, nor has it taken away their adult afterguard or their sources of trainees. It has organized two gatherings of sail training ships, in London in 1975 and in Fowey and Port St Mary, Isle of Man in 1979. It has produced a leaflet which enables prospective trainees and their parents to ascertain the addresses of the ASTO members and read a short description of their activites and it is ready to speak with one voice for its members when and if there is a need for such a voice, perhaps in the face of pending legislation or to emphasize the standards which are maintained throughout the membership. ASTO complements the work of the Sail Training Association (STA) which by virtue of its organization of International Sail Training Races, has thereby become something of an international authority and spokesman for sail training on a world-wide basis, whereas ASTO carries out a national responsibility.

Brave Benbow

Come all you seamen bold and draw near, and draw near,
Come all you seamen bold and draw near,
It's of an admiral's fame,
Oh brave Benbow was his name,
How he fought on all the Main, ye shall hear, ye shall hear.

Brave Benbow he set sail, for to fight, for to fight,
Brave Benbow he set sail for to fight,
Brave Benbow he set sail in a fine and pleasant gale,
But his Captains they turned tail in a fright, in a fright.

Said Kirby unto Wade, we must run, we must run,
Said Kirby unto Wade we must run,
For I fear not the disgrace, nor the losing of my place,
But the enemy I'll not face, nor his guns, nor his guns.

The Ruby with Benbow fought the French, fought the French,
The Ruby with Benbow fought the French.
They fought them up and down, 'til the blood came tricklin' down,
'Til the blood came tricklin' down where they lay, where they lay.

Brave Benbow lost his legs by chain shot, by chain shot,
Brave Benbow lost his legs by chain shot.
Brave Benbow lost his legs and all on his stumps he begs,
Fight on my English lads, 'tis our lot, 'tis our lot.

The surgeon dressed his wounds, Benbow cries, Benbow cries,
The surgeon dressed his wound, Benbow cries,
Let a cradle now in haste on the quarter deck be placed,
That the enemy I may face 'til I die, 'til I die.

TRADITIONAL

Chapter 3

Some British Sail Training Organizations

In this chapter I am going to discuss one or two of the British sail training schemes in some detail, partly because I hope it will be interesting, but also because although as they evolved many of their facets were remarkably similar, there are inevitably many major differences, and because there are more ways than one of doing this work, lessons can be learnt from each of them.

I will start with the London Sailing Project (LSP), because although it is one of the smaller organizations, it is one of the most successful and, in its curious way, it has lent its structure to many others formed subsequently. Perhaps I could remind you about the story of the bumble-bee; you will see why when I come to the end of the story. You may know that a Government inquiry was ordered on the bumble-bee and eminent aerodynamicists fed all sorts of parameters, such as wing area, beat frequencies, body shape, resistance due to hair and so on, into their most powerful computers; the answer emerged that incontroversially the bumble-bee was aerodynamically unsound and quite unable to fly. Presumably the report was marked 'for human eyes only' since the bumble-bee flies on quite unperturbed.

The London Sailing Project has a similar incipient problem because according to all normal parameters, it cannot function! I have stated its aim in the first chapter, which it achieves by the operation of three yachts. *Rona*, a beautiful Bermudian ketch built in 1895 and extensively re-built in 1951 is subsequently maintained at vast expense. *Donald Searle* is a standard Ocean 75 in hull and rig, but with the accommodation below decks, designed by one of the project skippers, Tony Sharples, and subsequently modified by the Fleet Officer Ken Howell, she is therefore a custom-built sail training ship. *Helen Mary R* is a Bowman 57 with a layout based on the lessons learnt from operating *Donald Searle*. So far this seems quite a conventional set-up. However, for every voyage of a weekend or a week's duration, there is a completely different crew, a new skipper, a new afterguard, new everyone and not even a bosun lurking unwashed and unloved in some hiding place beloved of young

Donald Searle's crew doing some serious entertaining.

bosuns. For three yachts there are approximately 60 skippers, and here is one of the strengths of the scheme: of those 60 some 28 started in the project as trainees. Thus they know the project and its craft extremely well and because they can put themselves in the position of a newly-joined and extremely apprehensive trainee they can understand and sympathize with that apprehension and quickly win the respect of the trainees and give inspiration to those youngsters who aspire to becoming a skipper themselves.

The project has a well defined 'pecking order'. At the top is the chairman of the trustees, who number about eight and who are the executive committee responsible for the policy and management of the scheme. There is then an honorary organizer, who, as his title suggests, is paid an honorarium and in theory works part-time — in practice quite a lot of part-time; he is the chief executive for the trustees and organizes everything, including making sure that there is a supply of boys to fill the berths. He is helped in the running of the project by the fleet officer, who is directly responsible for the maintenance and operation of the yachts and their boats which consist of a 24 ft and two 17 ft motor launches and six Coypu dinghies; also the land transport, a mini-bus and a van. The fleet officer has an assistant together with one lad. So the 'permanent crew' of the project is one part-time organizer and three others. Obviously the more they can do themselves in the way of maintenance —

painting, engine repairs, rigging, woodwork etc — then the more the costs are minimized, and to this end they undertake quite major tasks themselves without calling in the yard.

On board the yachts there is a skipper and he has a mate to help him who is responsible for the routine on board, whether at sea or in harbour, and is the deputy for the skipper. In this respect he has to be sufficiently qualified to bring the vessel safely back into a harbour should this become necessary in an emergency. Now because of the nature of the project he, like everyone else in the afterguard, is understudying the person above him, learning seamanship and gaining experience, so that in time if he stays with the project he will qualify for the next rank up. After the mate come two watch officers, each in charge of a watch of six boys (five in the small yacht) who 'keeps the deck' while his watch is on duty. Each watch officer is responsible to the skipper for the safety of the yacht during this time and also, at all times, he should be ensuring that his six youngsters are getting the most out of their time on board. There is space for a third watch officer in the two bigger boats. To help the watch officers each has a watch leader, and in *Rona* and *Donald Searle* a third watch leader is usually carried. This office appears in one guise or another in many of the other organizations and it is not as conventional and straightforward a post as, say, the skipper. I am going to elaborate a little on this role.

The easiest way to describe the watch leader is to compare him to a leading seaman in the Navy or to a lance-corporal in the Army. He is only slightly older than the watchmen he is leading, has been promoted from their rank and lives and operates amongst them; being thus able to see all that he does and hear all that he says, they can follow his example and can gain confidence from him when various things happen for the first time, such as the yacht heeling to a breeze or the land disappearing when the yacht goes offshore. There is a tendency for teenagers to be utterly convinced that old people of 25 years and upwards can have no inkling of the problems they are facing or the difficulties of the tasks which they have been given to do, but the watch leader can be heeded, for after all, wasn't he just a crewman last year? The watch leaders are chosen from the crews.

After each sail training voyage a report is written on each crew member and those that have 'given of their best throughout the six days' will be presented with an Amory Award, a certificate that states that fact. If the boy has done exceptionally well and, particularly, if he has shown signs of leadership ability, then he may be invited to attend a watch leaders' selection weekend in the autumn, where he is presented with a series of practical tasks to be performed before an assessing team of afterguard. If he passes and if he agrees to do one working weekend, one familiarization weekend (of which more anon) and complete one voyage as a probationer watch leader, then he has succeeded and become a fully-fledged member of the project, and has climbed the first rung of the scheme's promotion ladder.

Subsequently, usually after about three or four seasons as a watch leader, if he wishes to stay in the project and provided he receives the necessary recommendations from the skippers with whom he sails plus the required qualification in the Royal Yachting Association's Proficiency Scheme, then he will be promoted to watch officer.

There is no time requirement for the next step to mate; it just depends on the youngster's progress in leadership and seamanship and the recommendations that he earns from the skippers with whom he sails. Of course many do not make that step, nor do they all wish to, and some drop out as wife, mortgage and the two-point-four children begin to take priority. If, however, they do want to continue for promotion to skipper, they must have the recommendation of at least two other skippers in the project, be the holder of an RYA/DoT Yachtmaster (Offshore) Certificate and have the blessing of the honorary organizer.

In Britain, the most commonly-accepted system of training and certification for the non-professional seafarer is probably that of the Royal Yachting Association which has a policy of 'Education not Legislation'. Prior to 1973 the only well-recognized system of certification for the amateur yachtsman was the Yachtmaster Scheme run by the Board of Trade, as it was then called. This had been started in order that a register of yachtsmen whose competence had been assessed could be kept so that they could be recruited in time of war or in the case of any other major requirement for people able to command and officer small craft. In those days the candidate for an Offshore Yachtmaster's or an Ocean Yachtmaster's Certificate would be examined by the same examiners from the Board of Trade who examined masters and mates in the Merchant Service. They also had to pass an eyesight test and an examination in semaphore and morse. In all cases the standards were exactly the same as for their professional contemporaries, the difference being that certain subjects

Ken Howell and a crew member of *Donald Searle* collect their prize in Bremerhaven in 1986.

such as the law relating to cargoes, stability and certain other specialities which are not encountered in yachting were not examined.

Nevertheless the Yachtmaster candidate had to satisfy the examiner on some quite esoteric matters such as the correction of a compass mounted in an apparatus called a deviascope. Various magnets would be deployed around the unsuspecting compass and beneath the apparatus which would cause it to have a hideous amount of deviation. The unhappy candidate would then have to correct it by means of another set of magnets in an effort to remove all the deviation. History has it that on one occasion this proved impossible but fortunately the examiner realized that some extra force, either terrestrial or extraterrestrial, was being exerted and he stepped in to do the correction himself — with absolutely no success whatsoever. Both examiner and candidate struggled with the magnets to no avail, so the examiner removed his set from underneath in order to start from scratch again — yet there was still a large amount of deviation! It was quite a long time before the candidate remarked quietly:

'I wonder if that scaffolding outside the window is making any difference to it?'

By the time of the early '70s, the number of yachtspersons coming forward for examination was more than the Department of Trade, as it was called by then, could cope with and furthermore there was a certain amount of dissatisfaction because the examination was completely devoid of any practical assessment. Another story was oft told, that of the vicar's wife from Plymouth who, it was said, had never sailed in a yacht in her life but, after some diligent study, had easily passed the examination. I have always doubted that story because when I was examined by the Chief Examiner of Masters and Mates in Southampton, he soon had my entire sailing experience dragged out of me, warts and all.

A new system was devised, to be managed by a Yachtmaster Qualification Panel, composed of representatives of the Department of Trade, the Royal Yachting Association, the Sailing Schools, HM Inspectors of Education, the Association of Sea Training Organizations, the ocean racing fraternity and others, all under the management of the Royal Yachting Association. There was now a five-tiered system of competent crew, day skipper, coastal skipper, yachtmaster offshore and yachtmaster ocean. The examinations were to be conducted by different levels of examiners, the two yachtmasters' by examiners specially appointed by the Qualification Panel. The certificates were issued in the joint names of the Royal Yachting Association and the Department of Transport, as it was now called. In Britain, many of the sail training organizations use this proficiency scheme, requiring that their skippers hold a Yachtmaster's Certificate and their other leaders a level commensurate with their role.

CERTIFICATE OF COMPETENCE

AS

YACHTMASTER (OFFSHORE)

No. 00.18

To *John Hector Hamilton Esq.,*

WHEREAS you have been examined to standards approved by the Department
of Trade and Industry (Marine Division) and found duly qualified as a Yachtmaster
(Offshore), the Royal Yachting Association hereby grant you this Certificate of
Competence.

Dated this *11th* day of *October* 19 *73*

R.Y.A.
Cruising Secretary

APPROVED BY RYA/DTI
YACHTMASTER QUALIFICATIONS PANEL.

The project uses this scheme at its various levels and thereby
satisfies both its own management as well as those outside that
standards of seamanship are being maintained. If he is interested, the
trainee can be examined for his competent crew grade; the watch
leader must have attained the competent crew grade and be working
for day skipper; the watch officer must have day skipper and be
working for coastal skipper; the mate must have that 'ticket' and be
working for his RYA/DTp Yachtmaster (Offshore) Certificate, a
requirement for all the Skippers who can, if they wish, go further and
obtain the (Ocean) Yachtmaster's Certificate. It is a rule of the Royal
Yachting Association that the examinations for coastal skipper and
above must be carried out by an independent examiner who does not
know the candidate, and thus the mates and skippers are tested from
outside the project. At all levels, members are encouraged to go out
and sail in boats other than those of the LSP so that they can learn
other ways of doing things and in an endeavour to stop the project
becoming too 'inbred'.

So there we have the on board structure; a skipper in charge, who
must have a Yachtmaster (Offshore) Certificate, a mate who can take
over in an emergency, two watch officers capable of keeping a watch
at sea with a third, probably under training, two sometimes three
watch leaders who are the link between the afterguard and the crew
and 12 or 10 (in the case of *Helen Mary R*) young men undergoing
their first experience of offshore sailing. Six tried and tested leaders
and 12 novices is felt to be a sufficient ratio of experienced people to
non-experienced to navigate the vessel safely should each and every
trainee becomes *hors de combat* through sea-sickness or whatever, an
extremely rare occurrence.

You will have realized by now that this scheme is for boys only; this

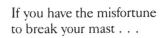

If you have the misfortune
to break your mast . . .

. . . use it for a fun-run
obstacle course.

Above HM The Queen meets crew members at Newcastle in 1986.

Right Captain Kolemenski (*Kruzenshtern*) about to collect his prize in Bremerhaven in 1986.

In 1984 *Canada Maritime*'s crew were all between the ages of 16 and 25 including skipper Paul Bishop.

Right The three wheels in *Eagle*.

Below *Kruzenshtern* — a majestic sight in the Gothenburg parade of sail in 1986.

was the wish of the founders of the project and is a factor which is reviewed at regular intervals by the Trustees who currently feel that the training in this size of vessel is best suited to either boys or girls — not a mixture. They feel that while there are more than enough boys in the Greater London area than there are places available for them, they should continue as the project was started.

The layout of the yachts has been adapted in the case of *Rona* and designed in the case of *Donald Searle* and *Helen Mary R* in the light of experience in running weekend and week voyages. Amongst the most important criteria is the need to separate the afterguard from the watch leaders and crew when required, and yet at mealtimes and other occasions to be able to get the whole ship's company together. For this reason the boats have a large open section in the centre of the accommodation in which everyone can sit together at one or two tables and can see and talk to each other. Opening off this area is the galley, large and functional enough to enable meals for up to 20 people to be prepared — and washed up — and a large navigation area (navigatorium as it is sometimes known) where, in addition to finding out where the boat is and the most efficient way to reach the intended destination, whoever is navigating can instruct those who show an interest in this speciality of sailing. Then at the aft end of the boat is a cabin which can be shut off and to which the adults can retire and, as far as the young crew is concerned, discuss the crew at length while drinking immoderate quantities of whiskey! They are usually wrong on both counts because there are many more interesting topics to discuss than this and most of the adults cannot afford the whiskey — although it does remind me of a letter written by one grateful trainee to thank Lord Amory for the opportunity to sail with the project in its early days. He wrote:

'We all arrived on board at half-past ten except for the skipper who arrived at eleven o-clock — drunk — as all skippers should be.'

This, not surprisingly, rather alarmed His Lordship until it was revealed that the skipper in question was James Myatt, whose extraordinary enthusiasm and extrovert manner could well lead an impressionable youngster to assume that his actions were caused by an excess of alcohol.

The rig, machinery, navigational equipment and many other facets of the yachts will be discussed in Chapter 6, along with some aspects of the ideal sail training vessel.

There is one paramount reason why the LSP system works and why it is so different from any other sail training organization in Britain; in 1986 the voyage fee for one week's sailing was £24! That was at a time when the actual cost of taking someone to sea in the yachts was probably about £220 and, believe it or not, that price included a coach journey from London to Portsmouth and back. Incidentally, everyone from skipper to trainee paid the £24. Now this means that if you say to a youngster 'If you're good enough, you can

Caught peeling spuds again.

sail a second time', you are offering something attainable and not
something which he will feel that he will never be able to accept
because of the cash problem. In practical terms this voyage fee does
not even cover the cost of a boy's food and coach trip, so where does
the subsidy come from? In the previous chapter I outlined how the
project got started and subsequently following the original use and
then the extended use of *Ailanthus* and the purchase of *Rona*, Lord
Amory bought yet another yacht, the 58-ft *Lily Maid*, later to be
replaced when she needed a great deal of work done to her by the
62-ft ketch *Dodo IV* and then in due course by *Donald Searle*. From
1960 to 1968 — and he would have been very cross with me for
saying so in print — Lord Amory continued to fund the Trust and
the boys were charged £9 a week at first, just enough to ensure that
they were not getting something for nothing and yet not too much to
stop those who really needed the experience from being able to take
part. It is, I believe, a fundamental factor in sail training that the
human animal reacts in a curious way if it gets something free. By
1968, inflation had started to bite and reluctantly Lord Amory
accepted the offer of support from another, anonymous trust then in
1980 the Searle Trust, which had given the money to build *Donald
Searle*, also started to help out. These three trusts, with help from a
fourth for items of extra-large expense, are the source of the subsidy
which enables the voyage fees to be so low, thus enabling young men
to sail many times with the project should they so wish and should
they merit it.

The project's year is divided into three sections. The sailing season
starts in late March with a fitting out weekend followed by three or

four familiarization weekends. For these, the complete crew is composed of skippers, mates, watch officers and watch leaders; it is their opportunity to sail in the boats without any trainees, to re-familiarize themselves with the yachts from how to switch on the navigation lights to how to reef the mainsail, from pumping the bilges to rigging the emergency steering, and every other evolution. Between the weekends, the three project staff get the chance to finish off any tasks that were not done during the winter. These weekends are followed by three more but this time with the usual on-board structure, including the twelve or ten trainees. Sometimes in the weekdays between the weekend voyages, certain organizations are permitted to take one of the yachts away, often with a crew of boys and girls, but always with a project skipper.

The second section is a series of week-long voyages lasting from early May to late September, and the crews join at midday on a Saturday until about 3.00 pm on the following Friday. This is a hectic time for the staff with a turn around period of only twenty hours. This is all very well if each yacht comes back to base without any major defect, but a grave problem if this is not the case. The sailing season ends with a watch leader selection weekend and a de-storing weekend, before the project goes into the final section of its yearly programme, the re-fit.

The final section is during the non-sailing season when the yachts spend from November to March at Universal Shipyard on the Hamble River. Up to Christmas the project staff of three, sometimes augmented by one or two lads either from the project or on a government scheme, undertakes maintenance and any reconstruction jobs necessary. Immediately after Christmas the working weekends start with parties composed of skippers (not as many as could have been wished for), mates, watch officers and lots of watch leaders. The work is hard but rewarding, and gives an opportunity for the newcomers to sailing to realize just how much is involved in maintaining and running a large yacht. It also allows a lad to feel that he has contributed something material to the boat which he can appreciate when he comes down to sail it during the following season. Often a watch leader will point out with quiet pride a piece of joinery or a re-wiring job that he has done. These weekends are fun, despite the hard work and often cold and uncomfortable conditions, and to the younger ones they are just as much an opportunity to experience the project ethos as they have when sailing. Soon it is March again and the yachts are sailed round to Gosport to start a new sailing season and give the chance to some 500 newcomers together with their leaders to experience offshore sailing.

The cruising area of the yachts is limited by two factors, those of voyage length and the prevailing wind pattern. Virtually every youngster sailing for the first time wants to get to France — it sounds different, it smells different and it cannot be reached by coach. Thus when he gets home and the girlfriend says, 'Where did you get to,

then?', 'Cherbourg and Alderney' sounds a bit more impressive than
'Swanage and Weymouth', which although delightful places, do not
need a boat to reach them. It is a project requirement that the crew
must have been on board for at least 24 hours before a yacht can
leave the Solent, the strip of comparatively sheltered water between
the Isle of Wight and mainland England. After that most skippers
make a bee-line for a French or Channel Island port, thereafter ad-
justing their route according to the weather prevailing at the time and
its likely behaviour in the future, aiming to be back in the Solent area
by Thursday evening for subsequent arrival at Gosport by mid-day on
Friday. Thus the itinerary for a typical voyage might be Cherbourg,
Guernsey, Weymouth, Cowes and home or, if the weather is helpful,
St Malo, Jersey, Alderney, Poole and home. However, there are plenty
of other ports which are visited, one helpful weather pattern allowing
a route such as Gosport to the Scillies in 24 hours followed by
Guernsey, Alderney and Poole, all in six days. The Skipper, who to
an onlooker appears to have a pretty easy time with everyone understudying his job and all wanting a chance to 'drive' the boat, actually
has a big responsibility to ensure that the crew work hard, but not
too hard, and that they make the most of their time on board. What
do you do, for example, when for four days you have had some
spanking good sailing with some steady force four and five winds,
plenty of sea time and the boat sailing really well, and then you
realize that day five and six are going to be windless together with a
distinct risk of fog? Or if for the first two days of the week you are
storm-bound in Gosport and cannot sail outside Portsmouth
Harbour? There are solutions to both these problems, one of which
is to give it to the mate as a challenge!

From time to time a major voyage is undertaken, usually in connection with tall ships races which the Project supports assiduously. For
example, in 1976 it chartered *Great Britain II* from Chay Blyth and
raced her from Plymouth to Tenerife to Bermuda to Newport Rhode
Island to New York to Boston to Plymouth, with a crew of afterguard
and 13 16 to 18-year-olds, prompting many people to comment that
it could not and should not be done. On the flight out to Bermuda
the relief crew were harangued with epic stories by two paratroopers
who had been in Chay Blyth's original Whitbread Round the World
crew in *Great Britain II*.

'You'll never manage it', they were told. 'It takes four full-grown men to
manage that spinnaker boom in a seaway.'

Continuous tales of gloom and doom were poured into the
unwilling ears of the teenagers. On the first night at sea, the door of
a locker under the galley sink jammed shut, but with a loud bang
someone managed to free it and release its vital contents:

'Ten full-grown paratroopers couldn't never 'ave done that', muttered
the happy conquerer.

Left *Great Britain II* — as
well as having sailed five
times round the world —
has found time to do two
transatlantic Tall Ships
races.

Singing plays a great part in
sail training, as does
meeting people from many
countries.

Their humour, although at times macabre, was brilliant. One
evening whilst setting the spinnaker, the 'four-man' boom slipped and
crashed on to a watch officer's head. The skipper was appalled and
quite certain that the man's skull must have been fractured. However
he lurched aft muttering about a sore head but otherwise apparently
all right. He was watched closely, but happily after a few hours he
still showed no signs of concussion or any other ill-effects. That night
in the ship's 'newspaper' — a daily broadsheet written up by an off-
watch crewman and posted on the galley noticeboard — there was a
cryptic newsflash:

'Today the spinnaker boom fell on Steve Burgess. It 'it 'im on the
'ead. Lucky it only 'it 'im on the 'ead, ovverwise it might 'ave 'urt 'im!'

In 1984 one of the project's own yachts, *Donald Searle*, was raced
from St Malo to Las Palmas to Bermuda to Halifax to Gaspé to
Quebec to Sydney in Nova Scotia to Liverpool in that year's Cutty
Sark Tall Ships Race. Other long voyages have been from Malta to
Gosport, while delivering *Dodo IV*, and some medium length races
down to La Corruna or Lisbon to the South and Christiansand and
Karlskrona in the Baltic.

I have dwelt at some length on various aspects of the London
Sailing Project because it is one of the organizations with which I am
very familiar. Having done so, I hope that many small facets of how
and why a sail training organization operates have been exposed and
may thus be of use to other people. The project's pioneering work
was copied by several other schemes when they started, and the one
that possibly used the project's system most closely, even though it
was adapted for the somewhat different type of vessel, was the STA
Schooners.

As I have mentioned, by 1964 many people in Europe were asking
why we did not have a ship of reasonable size to represent Britain in

the races which we as a country organized, and this was the spur which a group of people led by Hugh Goodson needed to decide to go ahead with the building of the topsail schooner, *Sir Winston Churchill*, and as it transpired a sister ship the *Malcolm Miller* followed in 1966. These two schooners, owned and operated by the Sail Training Association (STA) are quite different types of sailing vessels to the two 75-ft and one 57-ft yachts of the London Sailing Project, yet they have a very similar aim in providing a challenge and an adventure which will teach young people the benefit of co-operation, tolerance and how to live with their fellow human beings. If you include *Sir Winston Churchill's* bowsprit, she is 150 ft long and has a total complement of 55 people, and cannot therefore be thought of as a yacht nor yet operated as one. She is a small ship and as such has to be commanded and run by a number of professional seamen, a very different method to the bumble-bee related operation previously described. However, the first chairman of the Schooner Operating Committee, the forerunner of the present Schooner Committee, was James Myatt and in the early stages he had to decide how the ship would be manned, crewed and organized. Understandably he looked very closely at the LSP system because he had been part of it since its inception, had played a large part in its formation and knew that it worked well, so he and his committee adapted that system for this new and much larger ship.

Incidentally, the reason for the name of the *Malcolm Miller* is not all that well-known. Shortly after the commissioning of *Sir Winston*

The crew of *Sir Winston Churchill* waiting to welcome HM The Queen at Newcastle in 1986.

Lady Churchill being welcomed aboard *Sir Winston Churchill* under the welcoming and watchful eye of the First Master, Glyn Griffiths.

Churchill the son of Sir James Miller (a well-known public figure who had been Lord Provost of Edinburgh and later Lord Mayor of London) was killed in a motor accident very shortly after he left school. Sir James was impressed with the STA's new schooner and told them that he would guarantee the money to build a sister ship. Thus a second schooner was built and joined the first in 1968; a most suitable memorial to a young man who had died since her function is to benefit other youngsters.

These schooners obviously need a master, and due to the size of the ship he has to have a Master's Class 2 Certificate and the blessing of the Board of Trade (subsequently metamorphosed into the Department of Transport). The mate, or Chief Officer to use the professional rank, is directly comparable to his opposite number in the London Sailing Project except that he, too, has to have either a Master's Certificate or a Certificate of Dispensation which means that because of his experience and competence he has satisfied the Department's examiners that he is capable of carrying out the role of mate in that particular ship. Now come three new posts, engineer, bosun and chef. These three jobs are not needed in the yachts as their role can be carried out by the trainees under the supervision of the afterguard. However, on the large sailing ships it would be wrong and dangerous to depend upon amateur skills for the maintenance and operation of the considerable amount of machinery and electrical equipment, and of a complicated rig capable of supporting and controlling fourteen sails. Similarly there are few amateurs who could guarantee their being able to cook three meals a day for 55 people come rain, come shine and whatever angle of heel the ship may adopt.

'Six meals a day you get on this ship,' roared one chef with pride, 'three down and three up!'

So captain, chief officer, engineer, bosun and chef comprise the five members of the permanent crew who stay with the ship whatever she is doing. These five are supported by six temporary members of the afterguard and five youngsters who join for the same length of time as the trainees. These are a navigator, who is also a professional sea-going officer and, for reasons which we shall see later, nearly always the holder of a Master's Certificate, three watch officers, usually holders of at least the RYA/DOT Yachtmasters' (Offshore) Certificate which was mentioned in connection with the London Sailing Project and, finally, a purser and a supernumerary. The five youngsters, all former trainees, consist of three watch leaders, a bosun's mate and a chef's assistant (often politely nicknamed the Sorcerer's Apprentice and other less polite titles).

The three watch officers have a role very similar to that described in the project. They keep watch on the bridge whether the ship is at sea or not, and remain on board during the time their trainees are on duty; and they ensure that the young men or women get the most out of the voyage (the STA Schooners' trainees can be male and female but not both on the same trip). Making the most out of the voyage is extremely important. The watch officer is only responsible for one-third of the total crew of youngsters and only for the fortnight's duration of his particular voyage, so he can therefore get to know them quickly and, because he shares their watch duties with them, in much more depth than can the schooners' permanent crew. They have 39 youngsters in their care on every voyage throughout their sailing season. There is one other important attribute that the watch officer must have, namely the ability to work with young people, and this has to be discovered when new volunteers apply and before they are allowed to sail in the schooners; on one occasion a well-liked retired brigadier on reading a somewhat ambiguous question in the application form replied without hesitation:

'Absolutely safe with little boys, not quite so sure about little girls . . .'

When at sea, in addition to the watch officer on the bridge, one of the professionally qualified officers is always on duty in the chartroom, that is either the captain, chief officer or navigator. Whichever one it is will navigate for the period of his watch and is available should advice or assistance be requested by the temporary officer on the bridge. The purser, as his title implies, is responsible for all the monies on board and, at first, you might think that this is hardly a full-time job for an adult. However, it is the policy of the STA Schooners to give the trainees the option to bank all their cash with the purser, who then has to arrange for it to be exchanged into whatever foreign currency is appropriate and issued before shore leave is granted. Together with handling the ship's petty cash and being responsible for all bonded stores, spirits, beer, tobacco and also the mountain of chocolate bars and other 'nutty' and soft drinks that are consumed by the trainees, this is quite a busy job. He is also the first line of medical aid, the captain being the next.

The supernumerary slot is available to any adult who wishes to sail in the schooners and very often it is filled by someone who wants to find out what the scheme is all about and the effect that it has on the youngsters who take part. He has the job of helping the purser and generally assisting the captain and afterguard, and is also the unofficial entertainments officer should the elements and the sailing prove not to be sufficient entertainment in themselves. In the case of a girls' voyage, the supernumerary is a trained nurse, usually a State Registered Nurse.

Finally in this group come the three watch leaders, whose role is very similar to that of their counterparts in the project, and the

First time on *Malcolm Miller*'s wheel.

bosun's mate and chef's assistant whose titles are largely self-explanatory. Once again you can work out that of a total number of 55 on board, 16 people in the ship have sailed before and are tried and tested and able to cope with whatever conditions are encountered, enough people to get the sails down and the ship under control, although not to sail her to her best.

So there is the same thread of organization, captain, mate, watch officers and watch leaders, but necessarily augmented by other functionaries. The 39 trainees are divided into three watches of 13 and each watch is led by both a watch leader and a watch officer. For their first two days on board all 13 work together as a watch, but after that three of them each day become 'day workers' and spend the daylight hours working with the engineer, bosun or chef ('galley rats'). The consolation for their very hard-working day is to be allowed to sleep all through the following night, rather than having to get up to keep watch for four hours. On the following day they go back to their watch and a different three become day workers. This watch-keeping is perpetual for the whole time the trainees are on board and, in the case of the two schooners, the Royal Naval system of four-hourly watches is used. These change at eight, twelve and four o' clock with a 'hiccup' between four and eight in the evening. The first and last dog-watches thus formed are of only two hours duration to ensure a rotation in the timing so that the same poor wretches who had to keep the four to eight ('graveyard') watch in the morning are not similarly committed for the entire fortnight. If you find difficulty in working all that out, think of the unfortunate watch leader whose job it is to ensure that all the members of his watch are in the right place at the right time and that they are getting a fair division of the good and less good tasks.

If you have managed to follow everything so far, here is a final complication: whilst the schooner is at sea, the duty watch of ten trainees is split into the duty and standby parts. The duty part provides a helmsman, port and starboard lookouts, bridge messenger and note-book man — or woman — and they carry out these tasks for one hour and then swop over with the other half of the watch. After an hour on standby, they return for their second spell of duty and will have all been swopped to different jobs. Now you should be feeling real sorrow for the harassed watch leader! It sounds very complicated when written down like this, but in practice it is a good system which works very well and ensures a fair distribution of the many tasks and an efficient well-run and well-maintained ship. You can always spot the three watch leaders in the early part of a voyage, they are the ones working hardest, usually looking a bit harassed and peering frequently at their notebooks. However they generally do a magnificent job and earn the respect of the trainees in their watch and that of the afterguard. Without them the scheme would have to work in a very different way.

It may help if I list the sea routine of the STA Schooners but before doing so I think it would be helpful just to list the traditional names of the watches:

0000-0400	The middle watch
0400-0800	The morning watch
0800-1230	The forenoon watch
1230-1600	The afternoon watch
1600-1800	The first dog-watch
1800-2000	The last dog-watch
2000-0000	The first watch

You will notice that the forenoon watch starts at 1230 rather than the traditional noon. This is because it allows for a more even spread of mealtimes throughout the day.

0000	Middle watch close up.
0330	Call the morning watch.
0345	Call the chief officer and morning watch officer.
0400	Morning watch close up.
0500	Morning watch tidy up galley and PO's mess.
0530	Call the cook.
0555	Chief officer inspects galley.
0600	Call bosun's mate, cook's assistant, all day workers.
0630	Bosun's and engineer's day workers report to bosun's mate. Galley day workers report to the cook.
0645	Call the forenoon watch officer and the forenoon watch, purser, supernumerary, bosun and engineer.
0720	Call the captain.
0720	Breakfast for forenoon watch, bosun, bosun's mate, engineer, bosun's and engineer's day workers.
0720	Breakfast for chief officer, forenoon watch officer, purser and supernumerary.
0730	Call the middle watch officer, watch and the navigator.
0800	Forenoon watch close up. Day workers turn to.
0810	Breakfast for middle and morning watch and watch officers, captain and navigator.
0845	Cook, cook's assistant and cook's day workers to breakfast.
0855	Captain briefs officers in the chartroom.
0900	Officers take over the ship — trainees to half deck for chief officer's briefing.
0905	Clean ship (Happy Hour!).
1000	Rounds followed by Stand Easy.
1150	Afternoon and morning watches and watch officers, chief officer, purser and supernumerary to lunch.
1230	Afternoon watch close up.
1240	Forenoon watch and watch officer, captain, navigator, forenoon and morning watch officers, bosun, engineer, bosun's mate and day workers to lunch.
1300	Cook, cook's assistant and galley day workers to lunch.
1315	Forenoon watch sweep down half deck.

1330	Bosun, engineer, bosun's mate and day workers turn to.
1530	Call the first dog-watch.
1545	Call first dog-watch officer and chief officer.
1600	First dog-watch close up.
1720	Last dog-watch, first watch and watch officers, chief officer, purser and supernumerary to supper.
1800	Last dog-watch close up.
1810	First dog-watch and watch officer, captain, navigator, bosun, engineer, bosun's mate and day workers to supper.
1845	Cook, cook's assistant and galley day workers to supper.
1845	First dog-watch sweep down half deck.
1945	Call the first watch and watch officer.
2000	First watch close up. Chief officer inspects galley.
2330	Call the middle watch.
2345	Call middle watch officer and navigator.

In a similar way to the London Sailing Project, at the end of the voyage the captain will discuss with the watch officers and watch leaders how their trainees have done. This will form the basis of each youngster's report and will also determine whether they are considered to have done well enough to be invited back as watch leader, bosun's mate or 'Sorcerer's Apprentice'. If so, they can sail again at a considerably reduced price. Incidentally, these reports are only sent to the young crews' parents and to their sponsors, if any, so unless they are shown to anyone else by one of those concerned, the report remains confidential. Because the voyage fee has had to be a sum much nearer to the real cost of providing the berth than that charged by the LSP and because the duration of a normal schooner voyage is two weeks not one, not nearly so many are able to sail for a second time; sadly for those reasons and because they have to have a higher standard of seamanship in order to be able to keep watch in the 300 ton schooner, there are only a few who have made the grades from trainee, through watch leader to watch officer, although having said that, there have been one or two chief officers who have 'come up through the schooner hawsepipe'.

Because of their larger size and the voyage length of two weeks, the STA Schooners can cover a much greater distance during the time each crew is on board, hence a voyage starting from Southampton and due to end at London might take the following pattern. The temporary afterguard arrive on Saturday afternoon and familiarize themselves with the ship and also get some instruction from the captain and permanent crew. The trainees join at lunchtime on Sunday and go through the joining routine, being shown their bunks and lockers, meeting the captain and so on. Then follows an intense period of training while the ship is still alongside, including rope handling, sail setting, runner drills, yard bracing, helm orders and watch routines. Much of it is lost by the trainees in a welter of excitement and new experiences, but it has been shown to pay off once the ship leaves harbour, which will be either just before or just after lunch on the Monday. The captain is seldom given any precise order by his schooner office as to where he should go between the departure and the arrival ports, and is therefore able to make best use of the wind strengths and directions. Of course as already mentioned virtually everyone on board wants to 'go foreign' as soon as possible for all the usual reasons. It is also good at this early stage to get in a reasonable amount of time at sea, so if the weather is very rough it may be decided that after doing some tacking and gybing practice outside the harbour, a night spent in a sheltered anchorage may be advantageous. Otherwise course will be set for a foreign port such that a passage of 36 to 48 hours will be involved. After some two days at sea it is usual to spend at least 24 hours in the port thus reached, to allow a reasonable amount of shore leave and to let the youngsters catch up on some of the sleep they will undoubtedly have missed through the unfamiliar watch-keeping routine they have been working. By now it is Thursday of the first week and time for another sea passage of about the same length followed by Saturday or Sunday spent in a different port. This pattern is continued in a similar way during the second week, if possible taking advantage of the wind direction and strength, and also including a place of unusual interest where possible. I mean such places as Fingal's Cave, where a banjo and a record player have at different times attempted to render Mendelssohn's salute to an unusual cave; St Michael's Mount, the Farne Islands, Scilly Isles, Gulf of Corryvrechan or in France, say, the Rance Dam or Mont St Michel — many different types of interesting and unusual places. Finally it is usually planned that the ship will be within striking distance of the paying-off port on the night of the last Thursday and on Friday morning there will be the last chance to sail into the final port. The schooners usually dock during Friday afternoon so that cleaning, a final party and dis-embarking can take place according to schedule. Thus a clean ship is left ready for the next crew to join on the following day, unless their voyage is to be followed by a week in port for maintenance and various fund-raising activities.

The Schooners' year has three phases in the same way as the London Sailing Project. The year starts by sailing in mid-February on a 'shake-down' voyage which is usually followed by two other one-week voyages for which the age range for trainees is 21 to 69, and both men and women can sail together. Then follows the main series of two-week voyages — two fortnights followed by a week in port — until the end of October. The final two voyages in November are of one week's duration and are again for adults. Then both ships go into their third phase, the re-fit period, until their season starts again in mid-February. There is much to be done during the re-fit because as ships large enough to be subject to the need for official certification, such matters as routine docking, engine overhaul, mast, hull and rigging survey, life-saving applicance checks have to be carried out. All these procedures are also done on the sail training yachts but in a

300 ton vessel, to use an old-fashioned method of comparison, the work is harder and heavier than in 50 tonners.

Another of the better known sail training schemes in Britain is the Ocean Youth Club (OYC). Their aim was also stated in the first chapter and they achieve it in a somewhat similar manner to the two organizations just described although theirs is a youth club of the sea rather than an extension to the facilities available in existing youth organizations.

The Club was founded at very nearly the same time as the London Sailing Project and through a somewhat similar series of events. Christopher Ellis, who had been a master at Radley and later worked as a freelance youth officer in Stevenage, had started a project using an old, traditional yacht called *Theodora* to take groups of youngsters on offshore cruises whilst at the same time, an Eton master, the Reverend Christopher Courtauld, whose family owned a lovely gaff-rigged yacht named *Duet* was using her to take some of his Eton pupils together with some lads from the East End of London sailing in the Channel. They were both convinced of the excellent effect these voyages had on those youngsters lucky enough to go on them but they soon found that there was too much work involved in organizing crews and ensuring that the yachts were stored and victualled prior to each trip while at the same time carrying on with their main jobs.

The Club was formed when Chris Courtauld allowed *Duet* to be used for a season under the skippership of Jo Habens, whilst at the same time Chris Ellis was sailing his *Theodora* at weekends and for one or two summer holiday cruises. Jo Habens, who had been the Warden of the Sea Scout base at Marlow, then co-ordinated the sailing side while David Tonkin, the leading light at the Eton Mission at Hackney, ran the shoreside administration. When he had to stop due to illness, Jo took over both shore and sea-going responsibilities. They were assisted in those very early days by the Reverend Oates, son of the famous explorer. Once again it was principally the strong personality of one man, Jo Habens, who set the pattern for the way in which this new scheme would run. Thus the Ocean Youth Club was born, using *Duet* and *Theodora* which were soon joined by *Equinoxe*, the first skippers who had started off as volunteers, were made permanent.

Those pioneering days were very similar to the formative years of the LSP with sailing during the season and gangs of enthusiastic young workers coming down at weekends to carry out scraping, painting, rigging and whatever tasks they could carry out under the watchful eyes of the skippers. The new OYC soon found out the same sad fact that other sail training schemes had found; everyone was delighted that the youngsters should have this chance to work on boats and go to sea but remarkably there was relatively little public money available to help. The volunteers were obviously doing a fine job and enjoying themselves into the bargain — long may it continue thought the 'powers that be', but why put public money into such organizations when private enthusiasm and enterprise was providing such opportunities for the young? The situation has remained the same, although as the years have gone by and the Club has established itself, there has been a gradual increase in the financial aid available from government sources.

Between 1960 and 1968 the Club continued with the three yachts and from time to time had the use of others. In 1965 control was divided into three areas, Plymouth, Gosport and Brightlingsea and each area became responsible for its own recruiting of afterguard and youngsters. On board the yachts the 'pecking order' was necessarily very similar to the two schemes described already. A permanent skipper, later called a staff skipper, sailed for two-thirds of the voyages during the season and was temporarily replaced at intervals by a volunteer skipper in order to give the regular man a 'break' — usually spent in more recruiting and catching up on the paperwork ashore. To back up the skipper there was the mate and in those early days, there was a shore based bosun, Mr Strand, a splendid 'old salt' who had his Bosun's Store ashore at the yard and who carried out innumerable make-and-mend tasks and who was a great favourite with the youngsters. Finally there were the club members, usually 12 of them in a crew.

The qualifications required by the leaders on board are again similar to those already discussed. The staff skipper is usually not only a Yachtmaster (Offshore) but also a Yachtmaster Examiner, the volunteer skipper a Yachtmaster; the mate, who you will recall is often a volunteer and is on board for the same length of time as the youngsters, has to have a Coastal Skipper's Certificate, if he has not got a Yachtmaster's, and is likely to have sailed on several occasions with the club to get the hang of how it all works, probably having done a mates' training cruise; the second mate will be of day skipper standard and have a recommendation from a skipper and some experience of voyages with the Club. Nowadays there is nearly always a bosun on board, a continuation of that post invented in the early days and he or she is usually a club member who can afford the time to stay with the yacht for a reasonable part of the season, get to know her and her gear thoroughly and become an invaluable assistant to the hard-worked skipper.

The year 1968 saw a great change in the Club. Hitherto the boats had been old, the engines at times quirky, and in general there was a great pioneering spirit which was much needed in order to keep everything going. Now a man named Geoffrey Williams, a school teacher who had won the Observer Single-Handed Transatlantic Race, decided that the OYC was an excellent scheme and that he would use his new-found fame in the world of sailing to help it. He was appointed Director of Development and set about raising funds to build a fleet of purpose-built ketches, which had been designed by Robert Clark and to be built of fibreglass using a foam sandwich

method of construction. This building was unusual because the club bought a boatyard at Penryn, near Falmouth, and built the ketches themselves. Geoffrey persuaded a number of large companies to sponsor the boats and thus appeared *Scott Barder* in 1971, *Falmouth Packet* and *Master Builder* in 1972, and the following year saw the commissioning of *Samuel Whitbread* and *Taikoo, Sir Thomas Sopwith* in 1974 and *Francis Drake* and *Scott Barder Commonwealth* in 1976. Another of the family, *Arethusa* was also built and sold to the Shaftesbury Homes and was used for very similar purposes to those of her sisters at that organization's Upnor Adventure Centre. In 1976, its task completed, the Penryn yard was sold and the club benefited by now owning a magnificent fleet of purpose-built 72 ft modern ketches.

While this fleet had been building, the club had had the use of various yachts, two at least being famous racers, *Sir Thomas Lipton*, the yacht which Geoffrey Williams had used in the transatlantic race, and *Crusade* lent by Sir Max Aitken. Sadly *Equinoxe* came to the end of her economic life as a sail training yacht and was sold in 1973, her age being thought to be too great with consequent maintenance costs

Samuel Whitbread — one of seven identical ketches operated by the Ocean Youth Club.

Francis Drake — an Ocean Youth Club ketch.

for the exacting task of taking youngsters to sea. At the same time *Theodora* was returned to her owner, Chris Ellis.

With the new ketches came a slight change to the manning. In addition to a mate who came on board with the young crew for the weekend, week or fortnight's voyage, a new post of second mate was established. At first this was only a training berth and the incumbent did not need much technical knowledge, rather a great deal of enthusiasm and commitment. However, as he became more experienced and learnt some seamanship, he (or she) was able to share the responsibilities of organizing the youngsters and to help with the watch keeping. A young bosun was also often engaged, usually for a run of several voyages and he or she would live on board and act in a very similar way to the London Sailing Project's watch leader; probably having recently been a crew member, he would be in a good position to help, advise and lead the newly-joined crew.

With this new and enlarged fleet, the Club was able to increase the number of its bases and new ones were established on the Clyde in Scotland and Holyhead in Wales to supplement the Plymouth, Gosport and Brightlingsea bases in England. At the present time the

Club is thriving and has plans to replace the fibreglass yachts with a new generation of purpose-designed steel ketches. The founders and members from the early days sigh with nostalgia at the thought of how it was but are, I hope, happy with how it is, giving the chance for a large number of club members to get a taste of the sea with the good that we are all convinced this does for them.

These then are three of the better-known sail training organizations in Britain which are currently available for young people to sail with and to experience offshore sailing. They are responsibly run and have high standards of vessel maintenance and pay great attention, not only to the seamanship abilities of the permanent staff and their temporary volunteers but also to the ability of those people to supervise, train and counsel the young people who sail with them. Now this is a most demanding role and one which no one can sustain for too long a period. Just try to imagine how it would feel to know that you are going to sea in charge of twelve or more other people's teenagers; it is a very great responsibility. At first, although this is obvious to a new captain it is something with which he deals automatically, probably not giving it very much direct thought, although sub-consciously he is well aware of it.

After a while this responsibility begins to weigh more heavily, possibly the outward sign takes the form of giving less detailed answers to the many questions from the youngsters, most of which are very repetitive, or tending to over-rule a suggestion of visiting a new port in preference to going to a well-known one. Another factor which contributes to this problem is the constant changing of crews and afterguard at weekly or fortnighly intervals; it has to be done for a variety of reasons many of them already explained but it is nevertheless very wearying. I can imagine you wondering why, if that is the case we do not dispense with the temporary members of the afterguard and replace them with third and fourth mates; the main reason is that the enthusiasm brought to a voyage by these temporary officers is a good counter to the set pattern which the permanent crew will tend to establish.

There then arises the problem of what to do when the job begins to weigh too heavily. It is not easy for a young man of, say, 26 who has been skipper of an Ocean Youth Club 72 ft ketch for four years to find a job with the same sense of excitement, the same responsibility, the same opportunity to lead young men and women; selling insurance is not exactly a reasonable substitute! He may not have been trained or have qualified in anything other than this specialized role of commanding small offshore craft. Equally the master of one of the bigger schooners will find that the more conventional job which may be available to him when he has returned to his shipping company is a poor substitute for the sail training command that he has just relinquished. This is a very real problem both for the sail training operators and the for the permanent crews concerned.

Today's Monday

Today's Monday, today's Monday,
Monday is washing day,
Is everybody happy?
You bet your life we are.

Today's Tuesday, today's Tuesday,
Tuesday is S-o-u-p,
Is everybody happy?
You bet your life we are.

Today's Wednesday, today's Wednesday,
Wednesday's Roast-a-Beef,
Is everybody happy?
You bet your life we are.

Today's Thursday, today's Thursday,
Thursday is Shepherd's Pie,
Is everybody happy?
You bet your life we are.

Today's Friday, today's Friday,
Friday is f-i-s-h,
Is everybody happy?
You bet your life we are.

Today's Saturday, today's Saturday,
Saturday is pay day,
Is everybody happy?
You bet your life we are.

Today's Sunday, today's Sunday,
Sunday is Chu-urch,
Is everybody happy?
You bet your life we are!

Chapter 4

Sail Training in Other Countries

In some ways, the European countries have always been ahead of Britain when it comes to sail training, and they still are ahead. This is particularly so in the case of the operation of large square-riggers and the training of young entrants to their armed and merchant navies. It is a sad fact, which I have mentioned several times already, that Britain does not have a large sailing ship nor does it seem remotely likely that our Royal Navy nor our Merchant Navy will decide to build or support such a ship for training purposes. Throughout the rest of Europe, however, there has been a great interest, both in the past and currently, in operating these big ships and I give a more detailed description and distribution of them in Chapter 5.

It is in the field of the smaller sailing ships that Britain has led the way, at least since 1960. Most continental countries with a seaboard have had individual schemes to take youngsters offshore in small or medium sized sailing boats, but until recently there has been virtually no co-ordination of such training within the country and certainly not in co-operation with other countries.

In West Germany there has emerged a great interest in sail training for youngsters, where they have a very large number of what they call 'old-timers', traditionally-rigged yachts, both large and small, either refurbished trading ships or boats constructed in recent times in the style of these old ships. A number of universities and other sailing clubs have run yachts for the benefit of their members and the younger members in particular. For example, Kiel University has owned *Peter von Danzig* for many years and their members have done some noteworthy voyages in her; the 1964 Transatlantic Tall Ships race for one and, even more ambitious, the second Whitbread Round the World Race. Berlin University owns *Walross III* which can equal these long voyages with the 1976 Cutty Sark Tall Ships Race and the third Whitbread Round the World Race under her keel. In addition to the universities, the Clipper organization in Germany runs along very similar lines to those of Britain's Ocean Youth Club and London Sailing Project, and you could say that its organization is a mixture of the two. It owns three old sailing ships, two ex-yachts, *Amphitrite* and

Right *Carola* has done many Tall Ships races including two transatlantic ones.

Below *Albatross* belongs to the German Clipper organization.

Seute Deern and an ex-trader, *Albatross*, formerly named *Esther Lohse*. These three have a volunteer 'permanent' skipper who spends as much time with the ship as he can and is responsible for its winter re-fit and its general maintenance throughout the season. He will sail on some of the voyages, the rest being skippered by other volunteers. They have very high standards, at least three ex-captains of the *Gorch Fock* being 'on their books'. Another of their skippers is Professor Manfred Hovener who was the chairman of the Sail Training Association of Germany (STAG).

Now it is the policy of the Sail Training Association (STA) in Britain to appoint a national representative in all those countries who regularly support their races. In West Germany they were fortunate to secure the services in 1970 of Captain Hans Engel, one of the ex *Gorch Fock* captains referred to above. He did the job until 1981 and in addition he was a Council member of STA. During this time he organized the gathering of tall ships at Kiel in 1972 at the time of the sailing Olympics, and this did a great deal to bring sail training to the attention of people in Germany. Before he retired, he suggested to the STA that he be replaced by Manfred Hovener, a professor at the Merchant Marine Academy in Bremerhaven, a man with friends and contacts throughout the world of sailing and a keen exponent of sail training. Manfred not only took on the mantle of representation but went a step further and, with the support of a number of other keen sail trainers, formed STAG. Notably Captain von Stackelberg also a

Gorch Fock and *Dar Pomorza* having crowd trouble at the start at Gothenburg in 1978.

former commanding officer of *Gorch Fock* as President; Captain Hans Engle, Professor Harms, Dr Terheyden, Admiral Wind and the Hon Greville Howard as Members of Honour; Captain Hans-Edwin Reith whose *Carola* had competed in two transatlantic tall ships races and numerous others as Shipowner of Honour; Heinrich Woermann whose traditional yacht *Olifant* is also entered whenever possible, Harald von Forstener, skipper of *Tina IV* in the 1976 transatlantic race, Siegfried Schadageis, Paul Hertrampf who had shown great interest in Flensburg, Horst Jansen, Hans-Jurgen Krams and Hendrik Schadagies as Committee Members and I know that there must be several others who have a 'back room' job in the Association and who are therefore not so well-known but whose contribution is nevertheless a vital one. In 1987, Harald von Forstener succeeded Captain Hovener as Chairman and Admiral Wind succeeded Captain Hovener as STA's national representative.

STAG is doing a very good job of co-ordinating sail training activities in their country, bringing to the attention of interested owners of suitable sailing boats the possibility of taking youngsters out in their vessels and co-operating with various ports who would like to extend a welcome to fleets of traditional craft, but who need the introduction and also some guidance as to how to administer the

Gorch Fock passes under the bridge at Lisbon.

Olifant with a bone in her trunk.

fleet and how to make an interesting and educative programme for its young crews. They have set up a very good relationship with such ports as Bremerhaven, Cuxhaven, Flensburg, Kiel and Travemunde and are extending their influence all the time. They do a great deal of work in bringing international sailing events such as the tall ships races and rallies to the attention of boat owners. Currently they are working towards the commissioning of a civilian sail training ship by converting a former lightship into a barquentine. Many of the German lightships were designed on similar lines to sailing ships and were built to the very highest standards for, although they did not move very far, they had to stand up to very heavy weather when anchored on station. They were also fitted with engines and could steam between their depots and their stations, and although for obvious reasons these engines have not had many hours running, they were meticulously maintained.

A very similar Association has been formed in the Netherlands. From 1962 until 1985, Kees van Dam was the Sail Training Association's national representative for sail training in Holland and shortly after his retirement from that post, Bernard Heppener, a long-time skipper of the Dutch Naval training ketch *Urania*, took over the responsibility. In a very similar way to that in which West Germany's Association was formed, Bernard and a group of supporters formed the Sail Training Association of the Netherlands (STAN). He was supported, as was Manfred Hovener, by a group of enthusiasts who were similarly interested in the effect that these activities could have upon young people in their country, and amongst those at the front

Urania — the Dutch Navy's
sail trainer.

of the formation were D M Dragt, a Rotterdam lawyer and currently
the chairman of the Netherlands sail training schooner *Eendracht* who
was a leading supporter while the idea was being transformed into the
reality of an Association. A great deal of work was done by Leo van
Gasselt, an Amsterdam business man; by Gerry Ulrich the skipper of
Apollo and a keen participant in many international sail training races
and events; Martinus Kosters who was the first secretary, and there
were representatives of the 'Brown Fleet' which is an interesting fleet
of converted old-timers mostly engaged in charter work and owned
by a group of highly enthusiastic people who use the charter fees to
enable them to run the boats and maintain them as close to their
original specification as modern materials and safety requirements
allow. STAN has very similar aims to Britain's STA and to that of its
German sister organization. They encourage those owners who want
to take youngsters sailing offshore and they advise those ports who
wish to invite the sail training ships.

Holland already has a civilian sail training schooner named *Eendracht*, which has been running since 1970, which I mentioned in Chapter 2. Happily the story is repeated yet again, this time further south in Portugal. The first of the STA's Tall Ships Races took place in 1956 and I describe this in more detail in Chapter 9. One of the chief organizers in Lisbon, the destination port for this first race, was Engineer Luis Lobato, a keen Portuguese yachtsman and a man of considerable influence in his country not only as an engineer, but also as a business man and as a director of the Gulbenkian Foundation. He is also a rather special yachtsman in that he rescued the famous yacht *Jolie Brise* when its then owners abandoned it in Lisbon due to lack of funds and the fact that she was no longer in a fit state to continue their planned voyage to Australia. This is a fascinating tale in itself and is very well told in Robin Bryer's book of the same name as the yacht. Engineer Lobato was the chief organizer when the sail training fleet again visited Lisbon in both 1964 and 1982, and in between times he did a very great deal to encourage sail training in Lisbon and other ports in Portugal. You will not be too surprised to learn that he, too, was the STA representative in his country and he also decided to form a Sail Training Association, this time called Aporvela, meaning the Association Portuguese for Training under Sail. To achieve this he managed to elicit a great deal of support from senior officers of the Portuguese Navy, particularly his right hand man, Commander Luis Bilreiro who acts as the 'technician' of the association. Their aims are virtually the same as those of their sister organizations and they, too, are trying to get a civilian sail training ship into commission, the ex Grand Banks fishing schooner *Creoula*.

Eendracht is the Dutch sail training schooner.

Aporvela have taken a number of practical steps towards encouraging sail training ships from other nations to visit in that they have established some berths for such craft in the Doca da Marinha in Lisbon, which is situated near to the office of Aporvela. They also have an arrangement with the large marina at Villamoura whereby sail training ships are made welcome and given favourable rates. *Eendracht* often takes advantage of this during winter months, and in return she takes a number of Portuguese youngsters on her voyages sailed in the area. This marina is a useful stopping off place for small and medium sail training ships on their way to and from the Mediterranean.

There is a great deal of interest in sail training in Sweden. For many years the Swedish Cruising Club has been carrying out a programme for young people in their lovely old vessels *Gratitude*, *Gratia* and *Leader*. The last of these was sold recently, to be lovingly brought up to standard and operated again for sail training in Scotland, and to replace her they have built *Atlantica*, a new ship built to the old-fashioned but sea-kindly lines of a Brixham Trawler and a second new ship, *Tibnor*. Their aim and operation is quite similar to the Ocean Youth Club in Britain or Clipper of West Germany. They have a number of dedicated skippers who run the boats to a very high standard and provide the opportunity for Swedish youngsters to sail offshore, and like those other organizations, they have a promotional system whereby they can generate

The Swedish Cruising Club's *Atlantica* — a new 'old' ship.

Above *Tibnor* is one of the Swedish Cruising Club's popular and successful fleet . . .

. . . as is *Gratia of Gothenborg* **left**, with rakish lines from the twenties.

their own leaders. As is the case in virtually every other sail training scheme, this one was established by a splendid character with very strong principles which he insisted should be followed; perhaps the following snippet will help to explain what I mean. In this case the founder was Kjell Woller who was the fierce no-nonsense sea-dog with a gruff exterior and a heart of gold; a ferocious appearance which did not fool anyone for long, especially the youngsters. On a race around Gotland in 1980, we heard that *Gratia*'s generator had broken down and that the batteries were flat. The race support vessel closed her and shouted across to see if they needed help.

'No thank you,' Kjell shouted back.
'But you've got no electricity,' said the support ship's mate.
'No, it's a good thing,' came the reply.
'But what about your navigation lights?' shouted a worried, modern-minded mate.
'Paaaaraffiiiin,' came the one word reply, as *Gratia* sailed on.

Apart from the Swedish Cruising Club and the two naval schooners, *Falken* and *Gladan*, there was not very much else in the way of sail training in Sweden until 1980. In that year a great deal of interest began to awaken in the Western Baltic as a whole, partly, I believe, as the result of a series of interesting races and cruises in

Danmark — a good view of her square sails.

company which the STA organized in those waters. Visits had been made on two occasions to Gothenburg and on one occasion to Malmo, but it was when a race visited the small naval port of Karlskrona that a great surge of interest seemed to be kindled in the activity of youngsters' sailing. One of the town officers, Torsten Wikstrom, played an important role in organizing the events for his town while at the same time ensuring that the needs of the young crews were understood and provided for. This interest spread to Norkopping, a small but thriving port just south of Stockholm and from there to the capital itself. There are encouraging signs that Sweden may soon form its own association to continue to spread these activities and widen their scope.

Several senior officers in the Swedish navy have shown great interest in and support for sail training; Commodore Lennart Ahren was enormously helpful when the fleet visisted Karlskrona for the first time in 1980 and his successor, Commodore Lennart Forsmann, continued this support both while he was commanding the base and subsequently when he took over the post of the Sail Training Association's representative in his country.

Remaining in Scandinavia, Denmark operates two square-riggers, *Danmark* and *Georg Stage*, but these are principally for future merchant navy officers and their courses are of school term duration. Additionally they have a very large fleet of 'old-timers', probably even larger than the West German fleet, but at the present time most of the owners are either unaware of or uninterested in sail training activities. However, an exception to this is *Jens Krogh*, one of whose skippers, Bo Rosbjerg, has taken part in many international races and who would like to see more involvement by his countrymen. Certainly the international fleet has called at several Danish ports and has been very well received with the people there obviously understanding the benefits which the young crews are experiencing.

Georg Stage is possibly the most beautifully proportioned of the square riggers.

Right *Jens Krogh* from Denmark has very similar aims to many of the British sail training schemes.

Below *Sorlandet* — now mostly engaged in charter work.

Sunset and square rig.

Far left Two of Class A racing for the start — *Dar Mlodziezy* and *Kruzenshtern*.

Below far left *Guayas* from Ecuador heeling to a fine breeze.

Left *Libertad* on parade — note the lads on the yards.

Below *Zawisza Czarny*.

Right *Mir* — one of a dozen yachts from the USSR which take part in the Tall Ships races.

Below *Tina V* is a privately-owned yacht which takes on a young crew for the races.

Hopefully a visit planned for Copenhagen in 1988 should help to spread the word.

Norway has always had a strong interest in sail training but like Denmark this has mainly been confined to the large sailing ships. They currently have three in commission, *Christian Radich*, *Sorlandet* and *Statsraad Lemkuhl* of which more in Chapter 5. As far as small vessels are concerned, sadly there is much less interest among their yachtsmen in taking young people to sea outside their own families. However, happily there is one group of yachtsmen who are an exception to this and that is the Colin Archer owners; these lovely old yachts were all designed by Colin Archer, a British small boat designer who went to live in Larvik in Norway, and he designed the rescue boats which accompanied the fishing fleet on its long and dangerous voyages into northern waters in the days before motor fishing vessels. They are small and tough and deeply loved by their owners who 'found' the Cutty Sark Tall Ships races in 1980 and thus gained their interest in international sail training activities. Visits to Oslo and Christiansand were made between 1968 and 1978 but it was in Larvik in 1986 that the interest of the Norwegians was alerted to the opportunities afforded for young people other than just the sons and daughters of their owners.

In Finland, the fourth of the Scandinavian countries, I understand that there are quite a number of sailing vessels whose purpose is to

Colin Archer's son snaps Dad.

Right *Marietto* and *Liv* —
two of the Norwegian
rescue ships.

Far right *Kruzenshtern* acts
like a 'mother hen'.

take youngsters to sea, the Scouts in particular having some three
vessels. They are not, at present, represented in international circles,
but again the visit to Helsinki and Mariehamn in 1988 may change
this because a great deal of interest is evident in these ports and in
the country generally.

It is most encouraging that the heads of state in the Scandinavian
countries have all shown a great interest in sail training; I have written
elsewhere in this book of the King of Norway, who visited the fleet in
Christiansand in 1968, in Oslo in 1978, in the Isle of Man in 1977
and in Larvik in 1986, and in fact not only visited but also presented
the prizes, reviewed the fleet and started the race as appropriate. The
King of Sweden carried out the same functions in Gothenburg in
1978 and in Karlskrona in 1983; I understand that he would also
have done so in 1980 but protocol could not allow this as he was to
renew the port's charter the following week. However, his motor
launch was seen in the archipelago when the ships paraded out of the
port on their departure. In 1983 there was rather a memorable
incident when the young German crew of one of the Clipper boats
carried a huge stone up to the prize-giving in a net hammock. This
stone had previously been caught in the fluke of their anchor and it
had taken a two hour struggle to free it and therefore rather than
drop it back into the sea they decided to return this piece of his
dominion to the King personally. When the name of their ship was
called out to collect its prize, two young crew-members marched up
the steps carrying his property which they placed at his feet. The

Right The Polish *Dar
Mlodziezy*.

King was quite surprised (incidentally, so were the security men), but he bent down, gave it a little test and then, to the cheers of all the crews drawn up in front of him, he lifted the boulder waist high. In 1980 the Queen of Denmark started the race off Frederikshaven and Prince Henderik presented the prizes in Ronne, the main port in the island of Bornhom, in 1987. I understand that the President of Finland is to be the President of the organizing committee in his country for the 1988 events. Such royal patronage is important in helping to establish the responsibility of the sail training organizations in their various countries.

It takes many hands to hoist the Upper Topsail yards.

Starting a race for tail ships is not an everyday occurrence and one that demands some specialized experience. There is a splendid tale told of a certain royal personage who had graciously agreed to start a race, but when the time came was showing some doubt as to the exact procedure and how much was expected of him. The chairman of the race committee, sensing this doubt, came to his rescue:

'Your Majesty,' he announced, 'I shall come up to you and request that I should have Your Majesty's permission to carry out the normal starting procedure of the Sail Training Association.'

He paused and then added:

'And you will say — Yes please.'

Perhaps one of the countries most interested in the opportunities of offshore sailing for the young is Poland. For many years they operated the beautiful full-rigged ship *Dar Pomorza* for their merchant navy cadets, but sadly in 1982 due to ageing of the hull and main spars she had to be withdrawn from her sea-going duties. However, she was replaced by the *Dar Mlodziezy*. At the same time as running these big sailing ships, they have also operated some medium-sized schooners, for example *Zew Morza* and *Zawisza Czarny* and in 1980 they built *Pogoria*, a barquentine of similar size to the British *Sir Winston Churchill* and apart from her rig, quite like her. Thus they have a number of schooners and similar ships for young people and, in addition, there are a considerable number of yachts operated by clubs attached to shipyards, universities and other large institutions, in

Pogoria from Poland salutes her large sister.

which young people can participate in offshore sailing. They have a proficiency system and crew-members are encouraged to learn about their sport and become qualified so that as they grow up, they can take their turn at encouraging and helping the next generations of crew-members. The Polish Yachting Association takes this activity under its jurisdiction.

It was in 1972 that Polish sail training ships began to be more widely known, for that was the year in which they first joined in the international sail training races and began to form friendships with others involved in this activity. Two years later a remarkable Polish lady, Janka Bielak, also became involved. She had lived in England for some years and she came to Portsmouth at the suggestion of her brother, a well-known and respected naval officer and yachtsman who had commanded their Navy's *Iskra*, in order to help *Dar Pomorza*. At the same time she got to know some of the people in Britain who are involved in the running of the British schemes and in the races, and after a few years was elected to the Sailing Committee of the Sailing Training Association where, during the international races, she manages to carry out the work of some three people. To start with she speaks Polish, Russian, English and French fluently and, in

Flora from the USSR.

addition, good Spanish, and can apparently get by in any known language. Because of this, she is a vital link between people who speak those languages but are unable to speak English, and she works tirelessly to represent their interests during gatherings of the training ships. Added to her linguistic ability is a deep caring for the international aspect of sail training and what it has achieved in enabling young people to learn co-operation and, hopefully, through it obviating some of the misunderstandings and tragedy which beset Europe between 1914 and 1945.

Until recently it has not been possible to find out very much about sail training activities in the Soviet Union. However, in 1974 two large squareriggers, *Kruzenshtern* and *Tovarisch* took part in the Sail Training Association's Cutty Sark Tall Ships race; they seemed to get good value out of this exercise and the following year both ships took part in the transatlantic race which incorporated the famous parade of sail up the Hudson River in celebration of the United States'

Sedov arriving at Bremerhaven with her crew stowing the square sails; the staysails are still set.

The author emphasizes a
point to the Russian skipper
Valery Radugin.

bicentennial, and again this was a very successful appearance, so
much so that in 1978 the big class A ships were joined by a small
yacht from Leningrad, and year by year the number of entries has
slowly increased. Their sail training programmes are very similar to
those of the Poles, with the majority of the yachts belonging to clubs
associated with colleges, shipping companies and so on. As the years
have gone by, so the number of entries in these international events
has increased and good friendships have been formed between the
different crews.

In France, L'Ecole Glenan has been in existence for some time and
has a very good reputation for teaching seamanship to a high
standard; the Glenan's Manual is a highly esteemed treatise on all
aspects of ship management and handling. In my experience, that is
about the only French organization whose main purpose is to teach
sailing and seamanship to young people that is known about outside
the country. Sadly they do not seem to have much inclination
towards international co-operation as far as sail training is concerned,
although in the field of offshore racing, particularly with multi-hulls,
the French have a justifiably high reputation.

In 1986 a very thorough refit of the barque *Belem* was completed
and she started making voyages in which some youngsters were
included in the crew. However, they came up against considerable

difficulty with the government department responsible for ship management, particularly with regard to young people who were not professional seamen working aloft at sea. The ship is owned by La Caisse d'Epargne and managed by an organization named 'Deciders'. France also has an organization called 'Les Amis Jeudi-Dimanche' which operates *Bel Espoir* and *Rara Avis* and they take disturbed youngsters, many of whom I understand are drug addicts undergoing rehabilitation. However, this organization seems to keep itself to itself and does not appear to want to co-operate on an international basis. Even so, from time to time there are individuals in France who make attempts to establish sail training on a wider scale.

There is a small amount of activity in Belgium, Spain and Italy but apart from the large naval square-riggers such as *Juan Sebastian de Elcano* and *Amerigo Vespucci*, there is not much co-ordination of smaller vessels. Curiously, despite its location, there is a considerable amount of activity in Switzerland where the Cruising Club keep a number of yachts in coastal waters, particularly in Germany, and they encourage members, including young members, to go offshore sailing.

Rumania, Yugoslavia and Greece have shown a slight interest with their larger sailing ships but I do not know how much sailing for youngsters is practised in their countries, and certainly not very much activity is evident internationally. However, in 1986 the Sail Training

Amerigo Vespucci dwarfing the spectator fleet in Amsterdam in 1985.

Association's telex received what appeared to be the result of a computer malfunction; the paper was torn off the machine and consigned to the waste-paper basket. However, the race director felt that a certain degree of coherence existed, so fished it out again, smoothed it and sent it to Janka Bielak, whose ability to recognize any known language has just been mentioned.

'It is Bulgarian,' she announced in pitying tones, 'and they wish to enter the Tall Ships races.'

And so it was that *Kaliakra*, very similar in design to the Polish *Pogoria*, made the long voyage from the Black Sea to the North Sea and raced with the international fleet, very quickly becoming a popular ship.

Because those organizations in Europe of which I have some knowledge are operated in such a similar manner to those British ones that I described in some detail elsewhere, I am not giving a detailed description of their structure, yearly programme and so on. It is always interesting to me to discover that although formed and establishing themselves quite independently, most schemes learn the same lessons, come to the same conclusions and end up operating in very similar ways.

Left *Amerigo Vespucci* leading a parade of sail.

Below *Kaliakra* comes from Bulgaria and is a near sister ship to *Pogoria* and *Iskra II*.

Three Score and Ten

This song describes the effect of an horrendous gale which struck the east coast of Scotland and England at the turn of the century and decimated the fishing fleets of most of the ports on that seaboard. From Peterhead down to Lowestoft, each area has its own songs and poems which describe this same tragedy.

CHORUS
And it's three score and ten boys
And men, were lost from Grimsby town.
From Yarmouth up to Scarborough,
Many hundreds more were drowned.
Nor fishing smacks, nor trawlers,
Nor herring boats as well,
They longed to fight the bitter night
And battle with the swell.

Methinks I see a host of craft
Spreading their sails a-lee,
As down the Humber they do glide,
All bound for the Northern Sea.
Methinks I see on each small craft
A crew with hearts so brave,
They're off to earn their daily bread
Upon the restless wave.

Methinks I see them yet again
As they leave the shore behind,
Casting their nets into the sea
The herring shoals to find.
Methinks I see them yet again
And all on board's alright,
With their sails close reefed
And their decks cleared up
And the sidelights burning bright.

October's night and such a sight
Was never seen before,
There was masts and spars and broken yards,
All washed up on the shore.
There was many a heart of sorrow,
There was many a heart so brave,
There was many a hearty fisher lad
Did find a watery grave.

TRADITIONAL

Chapter 5
The Square Riggers

Whenever the phrase 'The Tall Ships' is mentioned, there is little doubt that it conjures up a mental picture of the great three or four-masted sailing ships which were the ultimate carriers of cargo under sail, the ships which had developed for centuries until they were eventually replaced by steam-driven ships during a gradual change over as the engines became slowly more reliable.

The 'Tall Ships' have many names, some like the terms windjammer or clipper describe their appearance or their performance; others such as full-rigger, barque or barquentine are technical expressions to denote the way they are rigged. In previous chapters I have described in some detail the medium of sail training and I have given descriptions of some of the small and medium-sized training ships. Now we come to the large vessels, the majority of which are used for professional training, to take cadets who are studying for a career in the marine (the fighting navy) or the merchant marine.

These tall ships can be four-masted but are more usually three-masted, although occasionally in the case of the smaller ones they may only have two masts. In addition to the masts, there is one other very important aspect about them and that is their yards, the huge spars which are mounted horizontally on the masts and which are used to set the squaresails. A ship is said to 'cross', say six yards on each mast. This method of setting sail is extremely efficient in terms of being able to set a large area of canvas for a given height and number of masts and when sailing before the wind but, sadly, becomes extremely inefficient when trying to go into the wind. Vessels with either three or four masts have similar names and the sketches show the differences between a full-rigged ship which has squaresails and therefore yards on all of her masts, the barque which is square-rigged on all but the after-most mast, and the barquentine with square rig on only the forward mast. In the case of the two-masted craft, there is the brig, square-rigged on both masts or the brigantine with squaresails set on the forward mast only.

There are many rather esoteric descriptions which are applied to

Ship

Barquentine

Three-masted barque

Brig

Brigantine

Topsail schooner

some of these basic names and a few have rather exciting sounding names such as an hermaphrodite brig. I have only given the more basic names of the rigs; for details of these other derivations a more specialized book should be consulted. The only hybrid I would like to mention is the topsail schooner, as there are many of these employed in the role of sail training. They usually have three masts, although there are a few with only two, they are not square-rigged on any mast but cross a number of yards on the foremast on which squaresails can be set almost, you might say, as an afterthought, because the basic method of supporting or staying the masts is similar to that of a fore and aft-rigged vessel, rather than a square-rigged one.

Have a look at the photograph of the Chilean *Esmaralda* and the Spanish *Juan Sebastian De Elcano* below; are they both schooners or is one a schooner and the other a barquentine? If you are not sure you are not alone, as many experts have argued over this problem. In my opinion *Esmaralda* is a barquentine because she sets staysails between her mainmast and foremast and does not set a boomed foresail, whereas *Juan Sebastian De Elcano* does, which I believe makes her a topsail schooner.

Having dipped into that little problem you will now see what I mean by esoteric rigs. In the heyday of sailing cargo ships, various other configurations were tried. The huge five-master *Preussen* came at the peak of operation of the great cargo sailers; in the United States where the schooner rig very much suited the beam winds experienced between ports, the *Thomas W. Lawson* was rigged with seven masts. Some say they were named after the days of the week. I

Two unusual cousins — *Esmaralda* and *Juan Sebastian de Elcano* from Chile and Spain respectively.

always enjoy the thought of the Captain turning to the Mate and ordering:

'Ease away Thursday's sheet, if you please.'

Goodness knows why, but that reminds me of the time when *Sir Winston Churchill* was taking part in the 1976 transatlantic Tall Ships Race and the captain warned the mate that they would have to tack soon. He, thinking to be clever asked:

'This afternoon?'
'No, on Thursday I think.'

Going back to the *Lawson*, the purists name the masts fore, main, mizzen, jigger, spanker, driver and pusher. I wonder how many dyed in the wool sailors have just learnt something; not, however, of very much practical use!

To continue with this very short and basic introduction to square rig, the names of the squaresails set on each mast are nearly all the same regardless of the mast on which they are set but, again, there are one or two traditional idiosyncrasies. The lowest and usually the largest of the squaresails are called courses, hence the fore course, main course and mizzen course — often just called the foresail, mainsail and crossjack or cro'j'ck (there you are, I told you there were some idiosyncrasies!). Above these are set the lower topsail, upper topsail, lower topgallant (pronounced t'gallant), upper topgallant and, finally the highest of them, the royal. Incidentally, the topsails and topgallants used to be all one sail, but as time went by and crews became more expensive to pay, with the consequence that not only did owners want their ships to sail with smaller crews but also the ships themselves were being built larger and larger, it became necessary to split these sails into two, in order that the smaller crews could manage them. These various sails conform to some logic in regard to their names, so you have for example, the fore upper topsail, the main lower t'gallant or the mizzen royal. Between the masts there are set a number of staysails and the sketches show the difference between, for example, the main staysail, main topmast staysail and main t'gallant staysail. The headsails, as the sails set forward of the foremast are called, are the flying jib (or it can be a jib topsail), the outer jib, inner jib and fore staysail. Finally at the aft end of the ship there is the spanker and its spanker topsail. The names are reasonably logical and once you have learnt the basic names, it is quite easy to nominate any one of the 35 or so sails on a giant square rigger such as *Sedov*, currently the largest sailing ship in commission in the world.

There is one thing that puzzles the uninitiated and that is the spacing of the yards on the masts. If you look at any photograph of a square rigger at anchor with her sails all stowed, the yards are in pairs with a very small gap between the pair, yet when seen under sail, the yards are reasonably evenly spaced with the squaresails set between

Above *Sedov* — a giant
among sail training ships.

Four-masted barque.

Left The spacing of the yards — at anchor and under sail.

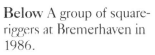

Below A group of square-riggers at Bremerhaven in 1986.

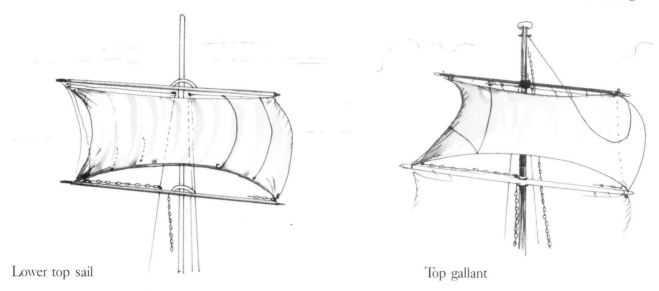

Lower top sail   Top gallant

Right Stand-by to brace the yards . . .

. . . let go and haul!

them. Obviously, therefore, some of the yards must be able to slide up and down their mast and indeed this is the case. The upper topsail, upper t'gallant and royal yards are 'running yards', whereas the others are 'standing' yards, fixed to the mast and only able to swing horizontally as, indeed, they all have to in order that the squaresails can be trimmed to the wind, regardless of the ship's course. Having pointed out this spacing of the yards, I should say that the modern practice is to have all the yards fixed as can be seen in the Polish *Dar Mlodziezy* or *Pogoria* for example.

There are two main reasons why these larger ships are square rigged. The first is that once you get a vessel larger than about 170 ft in length, then either the sails become so large that they are extremely difficult to handle or you have to have four or more masts, with the consequence of extra maintenance and loss of sailing performance due to an increase in the resistance of the spars and rigging to the wind, windage as it is called. If, however, you employ square rig, then you can have the area of sail which is needed to drive the large hull through the water in a form which is relatively easily controlled and handled. The second reason is that there is a very great deal of value that can be derived from the handling of these squaresails; the crew have to work both aloft and on deck and both lots have to work as a team both among each other and between those on deck and those aloft. In order to set a squaresail, the first thing that has to happen is that a number of the crew have to climb aloft and out along the foot-ropes on to the yard. There they have to untie the gaskets, the lengths of rope which are used to secure the tightly rolled sail onto the yard when it is not in use. Once all the gaskets are loose and the sail has flopped down, it is said to be 'hanging in its gear'. The gear in this case consists of the buntlines, leechlines and clewlines. All these lines must be slacked away when the sail is to be set and it is pulled down to the yard below by means of the sheets. If the yard is a 'running yard' then it is hauled aloft by

Haul away on the headsail sheets.

Stand-by to lay aloft!

Getting ready to haul the
Upper Topsail yard aloft.

means of its halliard (a corruption of the words haul yard) after the
sail has been stretched downwards by means of its sheets. This
hauling aloft of the yard is not quite as easy as it sounds, for the spar
together with its sail and gear probably weighs in excess of two tons
and the halliard is normally a combination of ropes and blocks called
a tackle, and although this increases the efficiency of the muscle-
power available it is at the cost of a great deal of friction in the
system. In the medium and large ships, unless the halliard is operated
by means of a winch, those crew members who are manning the
halliard, stretch themselves along the rope and then run down the
deck with it. When the leader comes to the side of the ship he lets
go and doubles back to the other end, seizes hold and runs forward
again. Thus you have a continuous stream of running, heaving figures
and this chain continues until the yard is high enough.

One or two of the yardsmen will have stayed aloft and, once the
sail is set, they will 'overhaul the buntlines', that is they will pull some
of the slack of the buntlines, leechlines and clewlines which is
hanging down the mast because otherwise the weight of the rope will
pull the squaresail out of shape. Very often this slack is secured aloft
by means of some very light twine which can easily be broken when
the lines are required for their job but otherwise they hold the weight
for the reason just given. Once the sails are set, some of the crew on
deck will man the braces, the lines which control the horizontal
swing of the yards, and trim them so that the angle of the sail is as
efficient as possible to the direction of the wind.

To hand, or as they say in America, to douse the sail, where
appropriate, the yard is lowered and then the sheets are slacked so
that the buntlines, leechlines and clewlines can haul the 'bunt' of the
sail up to the yard and spread it out along the yard, in order to make
it possible for the yardsmen to grab hold of its folds and roll them

into a tight sausage shape before passing the gaskets and securing it neatly and tidily along the yard so that the wind cannot tease at it and start it flogging.

You can imagine that while any of these manoeuvres is taking place, there are a large number of the crew heaving away at some ropes, slacking others, rope everywhere; the petty officers who will be members of the ship's permanent crew and who will have carried out all these drills many, many times, will take charge of various groups of the trainee crew and control and co-ordinate them in their various tasks. In most training ships, the commands to heave, to stop heaving and to turn up, that is to secure the rope to a belaying pin, are given by bosun's calls, a special form of whistle which can sound ordinary whistle notes, trills or in the hands of an expert a surprising number of variations of sound, all of which quickly mean a particular action to be carried out by the crew. Commands thus given can clearly be heard and thus obeyed, despite the high level of noise caused by the elements and over a hundred crew all scurrying around, hauling and heaving in order to complete the manoeuvre. Having described the setting of the squaresails, I can say that the headsails, spankers and 'tween mast staysails are set in a very similar fashion to those on a conventional yacht, the main difference being that the sails are very much larger and need some extra running rigging to control them; for example a downhaul to haul the sail down

Heave away on the braces!

when the halliard is slacked off. Incidentally it is as well to remember to slack off a downhaul before trying to set a sail otherwise there is a great deal of huffing and puffing from the crew and an alarming creaking from the downhaul and the belaying pin or cleat to which it is secured! To watch the crew of a large square rigger making sail is, to the uninitiated, to watch apparent bedlam out of which, in some unfathomable manner, the ship is transformed from a motor-driven hull to a beautiful sailing ship with its wings unfurled to the wind. Once this is achieved, an orgy of rope-coiling has to take place because each squaresail will have needed at least ten, probably more, ropes to be heaved or slacked in the process of setting it and all these ropes will have been thrown off their belaying pins on to the deck so that they can be used. To leave them there would be extremely dangerous as the movement of the ship would cause them to become inextricably tangled and then, when they were needed for sail adjustment or to 'hand' the sail as getting it down is called, they would not be free to run. Each rope is coiled neatly and secured to its very own pin, the position of which the young crew have to learn as quickly as possible in order that they can find the appropriate rope for a manoeuvre by day or night, calm or storm.

Having got the appropriate number of sails set and all their associated ropes coiled up and stowed, the ship can be settled down on her chosen course — if she is lucky! The problem is that, as I

Permanent crew always keep a careful eye open.

have said, these square rigged ships are most unhandy when it comes to sailing anywhere near to the direction from which the wind is coming. In a strong blow, they can only sail with the wind at an angle of something like 70° to their fore and aft line or, to put it another way, if the master wants to sail due north and the wind is from the north, then he may only be able to sail on a course of 70° on one take or 290° on the other. Then if you allow for leeway, the sideways slippage of the ship through the water due to the inability of the keel to entirely prevent this, you end up with an angle of about 160° between courses.

I remember an occasion when *Danmark* was sailing south from Plymouth to Lisbon and as is so often the case, the wind was not doing what it should have been in that it was from the south instead of being a Portuguese trade wind from the north. *Danmark* was tacking to and fro trying to make to the south and at one stage when she was just off Cape Finisterre, she made a 100 mile tack out into the Atlantic, went about and sailed back towards land on the best course she could make — to end up off Cape Finisterre again! Two hundred miles sailed and hardly a mile made to the southward. This is one reason why virtually all the training ships have auxiliary engines although, due to the difficulty of pushing the huge masts, their yards and associated rigging through the wind, these engines are not of much use in trying to get to windward in a strong wind or a gale.

If it is necessary to bring the ship about, from one tack to the other or in other words to bring the bows of the ship through the wind and end up with the wind on the opposite side of the ship, then if there is anything of a breeze all the crew is required. It is extremely important that, during the manoeuvre, the sails are in a configuration that will help the ship to sail up to and through the wind rather than cause any hindrance; in particular the sails at the extreme ends of the ship, the headsails in front and the spanker and its topsail behind, have the greatest turning effect. It also has to be remembered that the rudder, although essential to turn and steer the ship, also acts as a brake as it is turned and then presents its surface to the flow of water along the hull, so in practice the pivoting of the ship is achieved as much by the sail configuration as by the rudder. Another fact that must be appreciated is that as the great yards are swung around, much of the running rigging associated with them and their sails must be adjusted, and the buntlines and clewlines mentioned earlier may become tight enough to part unless the old lee-side lines are prepared; the yard lifts also need tending while the yards are swung round (braced).

Imagine the ship is sailing along, close to the wind but not too close, that is 'pinching'. It is time to put the ship about.

'Prepare to tack ship!' may be the order and then, when everyone is at their station and ready, the manoeuvre is started. The wheel is turned slowly and the ship starts to turn up towards the wind:

'Helm's a-lee!' comes the cry.

At this stage the spanker sheet is hauled in to bring its boom amidships which forces the stern away from the wind and, at the same time, the headsail sheets are eased so that they no longer draw, thus helping the bow to swing towards the wind. Soon the squaresails will start to shake, no longer able to draw and provide forward momentum to the ship. Now the courses, the lowest and largest of the squaresails, are brought up into their gear, left bunched up under their yards, which prevents them from coming aback, blowing inside out might be a simpler but less elegant way of putting it, and acting as giant air-brakes. At the same time the main and mizzen staysails are handed, for no better reason than this is the easiest way of controlling them from one side of the ship to the other as the wind comes onto the other side. By now the squaresails on the mainmast will have come aback:

'Mainsail haul!' will be the next order.

All the yard braces for the sails on the mainmast are now hauled or slacked in order to swing the yards around and the timing of this is absolutely critical. Too soon and the sails will act as a brake stopping the ship from moving forward and swinging up into the wind; too late and due to the pressure of wind on the sails, they will be impossibly heavy to brace round. Now the bow is hanging in the eye of the wind and the way is almost off or completely off the ship. Occasionally she may even start to move backwards through the water, in which case the wheel must quickly be turned the other way in order that the reverse flow of water past the rudder will help to pivot the ship in the right direction. Slowly she will, we hope, start to swing away on to the new tack and now the headsail sheets on the old lee side are hauled taut in order to bring their sails aback and let the wind continue to force the bow round. Ease away the spanker sheet so that the sail ceases to act, bring the wheel amidships so that the swing does not become too pronounced. The command:

'Let go and haul!' causes the fore and mizzen yards to be braced round so that their squaresails get a chance to draw and help the ship to move forward on the new tack, and all staysails that had been handed for the evolution are re-set. With a full and trained crew all this can be done in just eight minutes! In the early part of a voyage, with an inexperienced crew it could take the best part of an hour.

In some conditions, especially if the wind is light, the braking effect of the backed sails may be so effective that the ship will never manage to sail up to the eye of the wind and, conversely, in strong winds it may be dangerous to allow the squaresails to come aback because the whole rig is designed to support the masts with strong winds hitting the aft faces of the sails, and if the forward faces are subjected to great pressure the rig may collapse. Then the order is 'Wear ship' and instead of turning the bow up to the wind, it is turned away from the wind and the ship brought round in more than half a circle with the wind passing the stern; a successful manoeuvre can be guaranteed but the ship will have made a lot of distance to leeward (the name given to sliding downwind), not a happy situation when trying to force her into the direction of the wind and also a most unhappy situation in the case of trying to claw off a lee shore.

In many ways the wear is the opposite to the tack. The spanker and its topsail as well as the staysails are handed, otherwise they would tend to drive the ship up into the wind, whereas this time we want her to fall away from the wind. The main and mizzen courses (the latter sometimes known as the crossjack) are handed so that the wind can have maximum effect on the foremast and for general ease of ship handling and as the ship swings away down wind all the braces are used to swing the yards round, so that the squaresails are kept facing the wind. Finally any sail that has been temporarily handed will be re-set.

There is a third method of bringing the wind to the opposite side of the ship and this is called boxhauling. It is a development of the situation I described during tacking, when the ship inadvertently starts moving backwards through the water or, more correctly, makes a sternboard; in the boxhaul this is done purposely. It starts exactly as did the tack but this time the courses are not handed, except for the staysails and the spanker because they would hinder rather than assist this particular operation. At the point that 'Mainsail haul' would have been ordered, 'Let go and haul' is given instead, and the squaresails are trimmed across the ship which allows them to come aback and act as huge air-brakes achieving a sternboard. When the wind comes on to the beam of the ship (blowing at right angles to the hull), the fore and main yards are braced to allow their sails to fill and then the ship is sailed to complete the wearing manoeuvre — swung round so that the stern swings through the wind which ends up blowing from the opposite side to that at the start. The idea is that the distance made while surging up into the wind before the ship stops and starts to move astern is just about equal to the distance lost in sweeping down wind during the wear; in theory the ship will end up in exactly the same spot but with the wind on the opposite side.

For those alterations of course which do not involve either tacking or gybing the ship, one watch can probably manage the necessary adjustments to the braces and the sheets, and thus adjust the trim of the squaresails and the fore and aft sails. If you ever have the opportunity to sail in one of the big ships, when sail is being made all will appear total chaos and confusion. There seems to be no pattern to what is going on; petty officers are shouting or peeping away at their bosun's calls; lads are flying around everywhere, heaving on a hundred ropes in a seemingly totally unco-ordinated way; ropes are flung down on the deck like a giant plate of spaghetti; sails billow and thunder as they come down like venetian blinds or climb up stays like the sails on a huge yacht. Quite soon the frenzy dies down, the

sails take up their beautiful and efficient curves and the crew turn to
coiling ropes and restoring order to the chaotic deck. It is only then
that you realize that what you have been watching is not a heaving
shouting chaotic rabble but a well-drilled and well-controlled crew
who have set perhaps as many as thirty sails in a remarkably short
space of time. What is more they could not have done so if each had
not been aware of what the other was doing and helped if help was
needed or gone elsewhere to assist.

It is difficult to describe the orchestration needed to get a crew of
up to 200 people to achieve these manoeuvres; one of the best
examples I have seen is a small booklet entitled 'Eagle Seamanship', a
manual for square-rigger sailing produced by the US Coastguard. I
believe that there is a very similar booklet produced for and by the
West German navy for *Gorch Fock*.

What a remarkably old-fashioned method of getting about! Certainly, but what a splendid method of sail training embodying so
many of the ingredients that are needed. Some of the ships are
indeed old; the two largest, *Sedov* and *Kruzenshtern* operated by the
Fisheries Board of the USSR were built in 1921 and 1926 respectively. There are many others which were built at the same time and
are still in use for sail training, but ships of that age are now coming
to the end of their economic life. They are beginning to cost too
much to keep in commission, needing new plates, new masts, new
engines and so on.

As often as possible, the
larger ships open to the
public.

The majestic *Kruzenshtern*.

Happily many of the countries which use the square-riggers are so convinced of their use, both as training ships for their navies and as representatives of the country in other countries' ports, that they are replacing them with new sailing ships. This is the case in Poland where their beautiful 'White Frigate', as *Dar Pomorza* was nicknamed, was taken out of commission in 1981 and now serves as a museum in Gdynia. Happily she was replaced by a slightly larger ship, the *Dar Mlodziezy*, a new ship which has a great many modern fittings and methods of operation on board. For example her engine room is one of the most modern I have seen, but in essence her sailing gear is very similar to any other square rigger. The two large Russian ships will eventually be replaced and two ships very similar to *Dar Mlodziezy* are being built in the Polish port of Gdynia for the Russians.

West Germany had several training ships before the war and after the war operated one or two sailers for cargo carrying until, in 1955, there came the tragic foundering of *Pamir* which was carrying a cargo of grain and at the same time a number of cadets. Despite this loss and after a great deal of heart-searching, they continued with the building of a barque for their navy, and *Gorch Fock* was launched in 1958. She was constructed to a very similar design to a ship originally of the same name which had gone to the United States where she was re-named *Eagle* and is used to train officers for the US

Coastguard. *Gorch Fock* has three other sisters, or near sisters, Portugal's *Sagres*, Rumania's *Mircea* and *Tovarisch* from the USSR, although the Russian ship is now reaching the end of her sailing life. The Spanish shipyard Astilleros Talleres Celaya in Bilbao has built several large sailing ships since the war and all for South American countries, starting in 1968 with a barque built on similar lines to the famous five sisters just described, *Gloria*, which was launched for the Colombian Navy. Then in 1977 came *Guayas* for Ecuador followed by *Simon Bolivar* for Venezuela and finally, in 1982 *Cuauhtemoc* for Mexico. In other parts of the world new sailing ships are also being built; in 1984 Japan commissioned a new *Nippon Maru* for her Navy and New Zealand's *Spirit of New Zealand* joined *Spirit of Adventure* for sail training duties in her country. So although they may not sail very efficiently and although they may need a relatively enormous number of people to enable them to sail at all, they do look magnificent, they are splendid marine ambassadors for their countries and they provide an excellent form of training for professional seamen at the outset of their careers, and so happily they are still being built. Incidentally, not all new construction is being built for sail training purposes; as more and more leisure time becomes available, so people are looking for more things to do in their spare time and sailing in large ships is most assuredly cruising with a difference. In 1931 a yacht named

Dar Mlodziezy in her first year — Vigo 1982.

Simon Bolivar in Bermuda in 1984.

Hussar was built as a wedding present for her owner's wife. But what place has a yacht in this explanation of large square-riggers? Well this particular yacht was 353 ft long and sets 34,000 sq ft of sail on four masts! In 1979 after an extensive re-fit, *Sea Cloud* as the ship is now called started a new life as a cruise ship. Passengers can sail in her as in an ordinary motor-driven cruise liner, but with the extra thrill of sailing in a large square-rigged ship.

But what of life on board these large sail training ships? Firstly, these sailing ships need a far larger complement of trained and tested officers and crew in order that the trainee or voyage crew can work the ship safely under their leadership and can be trained in whatever speciality they are studying. A ship of this size and complexity is no place for amateur instructors, so the captain will have a chief officer and at least three watch-keeping officers. There will be a chief engineer and several members of his staff, radio officer, purser and stewards, bosun and able seamen, chef and cooks, with several other specialists as well. A large training ship such as *Dar Mlodziezy* has some 56 permanent crew in addition to the 154 voyage crew embarked for some three months. The permanent crew have a three-fold job, to oversee the safe sailing of the ship, to maintain her and to supervise and teach the youngsters. Of course as their period on board lengthens, the young cadets are encouraged to take over as many of the multitudinous jobs on board as possible.

Perhaps one of the great advantages that the square-rigged ships have over their fore and aft sisters is the opportunity for the trainee crew to go aloft in order to set or hand sail. Nowadays no one expects to report on board and be ordered into the rigging straight away. It is quite scaring for anyone to go aloft for the first time; you do not know what to expect, where to place your hands and feet, which bits to hold on to safely and which not. While I was mate of the *Captain Scott* we were often visited by mountaineers, some of them very well known and experienced in their sport. To my surprise most of them were just as apprehensive about going aloft for the first time as any of the novice trainees. They said that although they were used to exposure, their term for the state of clinging on to a rock face hundreds of feet above ground level, they had to come to terms with relying on man-made equipment such as the ratlines (the rope or wooden rungs on the rigging which, like a ladder, enable the crew to climb the masts), or shrouds (the wire stays supporting the masts). In a modern training ship, the first few days after a new crew join are spent alongside a quay and they are introduced to going aloft in reasonably slow time. As I say, the first time is scaring, but each time after that is much less so and the crew will soon feel quite at home climbing aloft and working their way out along the yards, standing on the foot-ropes. Very soon they will be able to work up there without fear, carrying out the drills I have described earlier.

Sea Cloud — a 'different' cruise ship.

Simon Bolivar salutes the crowd — Bermuda 1984.

These large ships tend to make deep-water voyages. The voyage crew will probably be embarked for about three months and, after an initial week or ten days alongside in the home port, the ship will make one or two shakedown cruises before setting off on the main itinerary. A transatlantic voyage may have been planned or perhaps even further afield with a European based ship voyaging into the Pacific or a South American to North America or Australia or Japan. Of course these ships have another very important role, in addition to their training tasks. They are, inevitably, marine ambassadors for their countries. To some extent the vast costs of keeping them in commission are offset by the goodwill and enhancement they bring when they visit other countries. There is no doubt that they are immensely impressive and engender a great feeling of excitement in those who see them, and a great deal of pride in the citizens of the nations who own them. Thus the Norwegian community in the United States, for example, is fiercely proud if the *Christian Radich* should visit a nearby port. It is this aspect of their work which has engendered a great commercial interest in their appearance, particularly if several of them come together as a fleet and if they can be persuaded to enact a Parade of Sail. It is highly important, in my opinion, that this commercial involvement of the ship be kept in perspective and not allowed to dominate the training role. There is a place for each but neither should be allowed to overwhelm the other.

Remember to keep your hands off the ratlines.

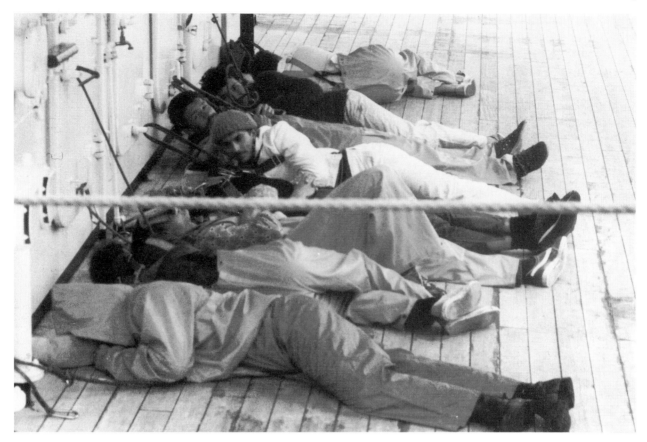

Snatching a quick rest between watch duties.

Life for the young cadets on these large sailing ships is rather different than for those on the smaller ships that I have described in previous chapters. As I have said, these youngsters are probably starting a career at sea and therefore they have an interest in the technicalities of sea-going. We have seen a glimpse of how the sails are handled and have discovered that for major manoeuvres, probably all hands will be required. In addition to sail drills, there are the usual jobs of steering, keeping lookout and all the regular routines of watch-keeping but because these crew members will continue at sea, they can be taught to carry out many more functions, jobs usually undertaken by the ships' officers in the smaller vessels. Navigation is one important subject and many of these ships have two navigation stations, one for the officer of the watch and a second for the cadet navigator who will do all the routine plotting and position fixing. At the present time there is a lot to learn because we are rapidly moving into the era of sophisticated and highly accurate electronic position fixing devices such as satellite navigators, Loran and Decca. However, it is considered extremely important that those new to the sea should continue to master the old-fashioned methods of fixing the ship's position, such skills as using the sextant to measure the altitude of sun, planets and stars and hence deriving a position and also the business of dead reckoning or determining the position by means of plotting the course steered and the distance run. These are 'fall back' methods which may well have to be used if the electronic devices fail. Someone once pointed out in conversation that the environment of a relatively small vessel at sea is a more cruel one for electronic instruments than that which they would encounter if they were fired to the moon. When the cadets are not required for watch-keeping they will frequently find themselves in a classroom on board, learning these navigational skills which they can then put into practice. In all other departments of the ship, in the galley, the engine room, the radio room, cadets will be learning from the ship's permanent crew and as the voyage progresses it is the cadets who will gradually take

An acre of canvas needs a lot of maintenance.

Sail setting appears to be chaotic but is in fact a well-planned and well-rehearsed exercise in teamwork.

over most of the running of the ship, with their instructors merely supervising them and stepping in to put things right if that is required.

Very often some of the more traditional skills will be taught; rope work and working with wire, learning to splice or make an eye or sail-making or any of the work of the bosun, the man responsible for the maintenance of the spars and rigging.

Boatwork is another important aspect of the cadets' training. In these present times it is becoming less and less common for a seaman to have to handle a small boat, even more rare to have to propel it by oars. These large sailing ships all carry quite a variety of boats and very often some of them will be propelled by oars, five or more all to be synchronized and pulled together — if the boat is to get where it is intended it should. The correct lowering and raising of the boats are excellent examples of seamanship and, in addition, are excellent opportunities for the cadet leaders to take charge of a relatively simple task but one which needs a leader to co-ordinate it. I have heard it expressed several times that unless steps are taken to correct it, the present day ship's officer may never have acquired a feel for the effect of wind and tide on a small boat; and this has become noticeable when such as oil-rig support vessels have to be manoeuvred in close proximity to a rig, perhaps carefully positioned to load or offload an awkward item. Those that have handled small craft, bringing them alongside the parent ship in a seaway or manoeuvring in a tidal stream, will always be better qualified on a larger vessel probably equipped with an air-conditioned bridge in which to hide from the elements.

But whatever instruction is taking place on board with the ship under way, there is always the chance that there will be a call to 'Sailing Stations' in order to carry out some evolution. Then lessons have to be abandoned and a rush made for whatever rope has to be pulled or sail has to be handled. I remember well one party which I was lucky enough to attend, on the quarter deck of *Gorch Fock*, with the awning rigged, bright flags hung around the inside and a splendid array of food and drink. As I collected a drink from a smart steward I realized that only some sixty minutes before, the ship had been under full sail in the river Weser, taking part in a Parade of Sail.

'What were you doing one hour ago?' I asked the steward.

'I was on the main royal yard stowing the sail,' he said and I could see that he was pleased that at least one guest realized that he had duties other than serving drinks. The teamwork needed to change the ship from a three-masted barque under full sail, to stow those sails, bring her through the lock, secure her alongside, rig the gangways, rig the awning and lay out the party was extremely impressive.

Away, Away with Rum

CHORUS
Away, away with rum, by gum, with rum, by gum,
With r-um, by gum. Away, away with rum by gum,
It's the song of the Salvation Army.

We never eat fruitcake, 'cos fruitcake has rum,
And one little mouthful turns a man to a bum,
Can you imagine a sorrier sight?
Than a man eating fruitcake, just to get tight!

We never eat biscuits, 'cos biscuits have yeast,
And one little mouthful turns a man to a beast,
Can you imagine the utter disgrace?
To be found in the gutter with crumbs on your face!

We never eat wine gums, 'cos wine gums have port,
And one little wine gum makes a girl easy sport,
Can you imagine a feebler excuse?
It was only one wine gum that made me so loose!

Chapter 6

The Ideal Vessel

Quick answer? There isn't one. Of course it depends on what kind of sail training you are going to do. The main considerations must be:

The type of training which is to be undertaken;
The number of trainees to be accommodated;
The age of the trainees;
The length of time they will be on board;
The areas in which the vessel will work;
The financial considerations.

Many of these factors are inter-dependent as will be seen as they are examined.

Firstly let us look at the type of training which is to be undertaken. This varies, but the following short descriptions cover most of the uses to which sail training ships are put throughout the world. Many countries have a sailing ship which they use in order to train professional seafarers, either officers or ratings, and for either their Armed Navy or their Merchant Navy. These usually large ships also act as prestige ships for their owners. For example, *Gorch Fock* owned by the Federal German Navy is used as part of the Flensburg Naval Academy to train future officers in the Federal German Navy, *Sagres* does the same job for Portugal, while *Kruzenshtern* is operated by the Fisheries Board of the USSR for training future officers and men in their fishing fleets. In Norway, *Christian Radich* is used to take boys and girls to sea as part of their ordinary schooling, and while they will not necessarily eventually go into the merchant navy, it is likely; in Denmark *Danmark* and *Georg Stage* are used for the same purpose.

There are a few 'windjammers' which operate for charter. *Sorlandet* from Norway and *Sea Cloud* which is German owned and registered in the Cayman Islands are not involved in sail training, for the kind of people who can afford to go on board for a cruise have almost certainly had their characters trained a great many years before!

The next group is the smaller training ships but those still used for professionals, such yachts as *Adventure* owned by the Royal Navy and used for adventure training. As a matter of interest *Adventure* took

France's *Belle Poule* looking
          for her sister *Etoile*.

part in the first two Whitbread Round the World races, which must
have been a *real* adventure. The Dutch and Portuguese have similar
yachts, *Urania* and *Vega* respectively. In Sweden and in France they
operate schooners which are far larger than the yachts just
mentioned, but not nearly as big as the 'windjammers', namely
Gladan and *Falken*, and *Belle Poule* and *L'Etoile*. Again, some
merchant navy schools operate such large yachts, *Halcyon* of the
Southampton College of Maritime Studies or *Sparta* of the Leningrad
Maritime Academy.

Yet another group is those ships which are run by universities and
similar establishments to carry out oceanographic surveys and the
study of marine life. There are several such ships in the United States
of America, including the schooner *Westward* operated by SEA, the
Sea Education Association Incorporated, *Regina Maris*, recently sold
and replaced by a new schooner owned by the Ocean Research and
Education Society and run with great style by Dr George Nicholls,
and *Zenobe Gramme* of the Belgian Navy which had a large marine
laboratory on board.

Then there is a large number of ships, both large and small, used
for 'one time' sail training experience. Many of these I have discussed
already at some length: the London Sailing Project, STA Schooners,
the Ocean Youth Club fleets and their counterparts in other
countries.

These then are a few of the different types of training which a
vessel might be designed to carry out. Perhaps the next most
important criterion is the number of trainees which it is intended
should be carried, which is very largely determined by the role of the

ship and whether it is to be financed by the state or privately. Here there are probably three basic groups. The 'windjammers' already referred to have to be virtually run by the state concerned and can give training to between 200 and 300 cadets with a permanent crew of 40 to 50. They are inevitably enormously expensive to run. A more workable size is the ship of between 100 and 200 ft on deck, able to accommodate between 35 and 55 cadets with the appropriate ratio of instructors. The third group is the sail training yacht of either some 45 ft or 75 ft length on deck, which can carry, say, 6 or 12 cadets. Once again the factors under discussion are all linked, because the number of trainees that can be accommodated in a vessel of given size must depend on what they are going to be taught while they are on board and for how long and how far the vessels will voyage.

Dealing with the matter of trainees' ages, let us start by looking at the low limit. It has been generally determined in a large number of different countries that on average the lowest age that can gain from this form of training is 16. Now some people will strongly disagree with this, saying that it is wrong to deny the opportunity to youngsters under 16. The problem is that all the organizations must deal with the average teenager, although of course there are youngsters who have done an immense amount of sailing, have crossed oceans and know more about sailing than many adult skippers. I am reminded of two schooners, *Te Vega* and *Te Quest*, which used to be operated by the Flint school afloat, from the USA. They came across to Europe in 1972 and entered the Sail Training Association's race from Copenhagen to Gdynia. Unfortunately there

The schooner *Falken* and the barquentine *Kaliakra* stand out at the start of one of the 1987 races.

were a number of boys very much younger than 16 on board and the race rules required that they may not sail on the race. As they stood on the quayside watching their school and their temporary home sail away, one said:

'Why can't we race? We've just come across the Atlantic Ocean and covered over 3,000 miles under sail. Why aren't we allowed to sail 400 miles in the Baltic?'

It was a heart-rending question and one that could not truly be explained to boys of that age. Those boys were an exception, but you have to make rules for the average case, and the average 15-year-old finds it difficult to cope with more than one night at a time with broken sleep. They have far more keenness but quite a lot less stamina than their slightly older brothers and sisters.

There are many schemes which take 13 to 15-year-olds offshore sailing, but their voyage lengths and the times between ports are carefully graded to allow for this younger age group. There is also the problem of mixing the ages; what is fun for a 12-year-old is often a crashing bore for a boy of 16, and the 16-year-old's fun is, or should be, different from the 20-year-old's. Thus the crew of trainees should be composed of groups of young people of a similar age range. These ranges tend to be 13 to 15 (quite an unusual group for the reasons just explained); 16 to 19 which is a very common group, for it is to this age group that sail training seems to have the maximum appeal and probably the best effect; then there is the 20 to 24 age group which tends to be those young men or women who are undergoing professional maritime training.

The length of time that the young people spend on board is an important factor in deciding on the ideal vessel for the job. Starting with the professionals, very often their courses are one term out of a year's curriculum and are therefore of about three months' duration. The two other most usual voyage lengths are two weeks and one week. If the youngsters are still at school, then the school from which they have been released, or, if they have left school, their employers, will probably be reluctant to spare them for longer than two weeks, so this then is a good length of course for the medium-sized training ship, in the 100 to 200 ft bracket; a week's course is an ideal length in the small 45 to 70 footers. There are two reasons why these course lengths have come to be related with boat length. Firstly, in the boats up to 70 ft length, all those on board, be they adult or youngster, are very much thrown on top of each other; the ship is small, usually everyone eats their meals together around one table and thus they can get to know each other quickly. In the larger ships this is not the case; because of the size of the ship and because of the need to operate a more rigid routine, the afterguard tend to take their meals in a separate part of the ship to the youngsters, there are many more people on board and so it takes longer to get to know everyone. Thus the spell which we hope that sail training will weave takes a little longer to work in groups of, say, 12 than it does with watches of six.

Naturally those organizations which usually run voyages of a week's length and those whose voyages last for two weeks have each tried alternatives, but have eventually come to very similar decisions. To start with, a week in a 75 ft or a smaller yacht is almost certainly the shortest time in which a crew can be welded together as a group of young people who will work together as a team, and whose individual members will get value out of the voyage. In the medium ships, this same process takes two weeks to achieve. Although every crew, like every individual, quickly establishes its own identity — a quiet crew, a singing crew, a happy crew, a difficult crew — it does take time for this pattern to manifest itself. When the individual young people arrive they are understandably nervous; they do not know what they have let themselves in for, they do not know the ship's officers, the ship's routine, how to sort out the jumble of ropes, each other — there is a welter of new experiences to be learnt. As a result they are shy and withdrawn, and most will keep very quiet rather than risk making a fool of themselves. When they sit down together for their first meal it is painful to watch their shyness and sad to experience the rather glum silence that exists; so different from a few meals later when the racket is almost painful.

To overcome this shyness and, in the cases of the younger ones,

Don't talk to the man on the wheel!

Bring your own jazz band —
Liv's crew.

homesickness, the youngsters are kept busy from the moment they arrive. They will be shown their bunk and locker, told to unpack and get changed into working gear and a training programme will start as soon as possible. At the end of this first, hectic day when it is time to turn in they are tired and, if the instruction and briefing have been done well, they will be looking forward to a busy tomorrow. On the second day, as they start to make friends with their watchmates and others in the crew, they will start to gain confidence in their watch leader and the other officers. They will gain confidence but it will take them several attempts at setting the sails and stowing them again before confidence in the gear is achieved.

Now in the smaller craft, because there are only, say, a total of 17 people on board and perhaps only four or five sails which can be set at the same time, this phase is over by the end of the second day on board. Then there usually follows a longish passage which may be marred by seasickness, followed by the arrival at a foreign port and an immediate resurgence of interest. In the medium-sized ship, this process takes longer than two or three days. There may be some 55 people on board, some of them rather remote figures not often seen, and there may be 12 or 13 sails which can be set simultaneously, each with a number of ropes to hoist, hand and control them. The ship's routine is necessarily more complicated, the whole business of settling down on board takes longer, and as a result the crew identity is not forged from its individual members until about the fifth or sixth day, that is until the end of the second longish passage at sea and the second spell in harbour. Now you will see why the smaller yacht needs at least a week to make the experience a worthwhile one and two weeks is needed in the larger ship.

Having discussed what I believe to be the *optimum* length of a voyage, now let us consider the *maximum* length. Those schemes which base their voyage length on six or seven days have all tried the experiment of running for longer periods and nearly all have come up with the same answer, which is that the amount of benefit which the youngsters get during the second week is minimal compared with that of the first. The reason for this is not so easy to fathom, but it is likely to be that during the initial period on board there are a mass of basic skills that have to be mastered in order that the mooring lines can be let go, the sails hoisted, the watch kept and the ship generally operated in a safe manner. All these tasks are fairly elementary, demanding a certain amount of common sense but not too much technical knowledge and, to one who has never been to sea before, it is all new and undoubtedly exciting. At the same time as learning to work the ship, there are new friends to be made.

Now if these young crew members are only to be on board for a general taste of sea-going rather than part of the general seamanship instruction, there is a limit to what they can be taught. The old description of a new deck-hand's education was described shortly as being the ability to 'Hand, reef and steer'. These are the basics, but if

Even quite small tasks involve teamwork.

the teaching is extended to navigation, meteorology, bosunry, communications and so on, then the youngster will enter a new level of instruction, and due to their specializations these subjects cannot be taught in a matter of days, but take weeks or even months. Therefore once the basics have been mastered it is not practical to go on to the next stages unless a much longer voyage is undertaken or unless the individual is likely to sail with the organization on many future occasions, but if only the basic attributes of a deck-hand are taught and practised then there is a great risk that boredom will set in. The novelty of setting and stowing sails, steering, keeping lookout and all the routine duties of a watchkeeper wears off and the drudgery of cooking, washing up, cleaning the ship and such domestic duties become matters of discontent. It has been found by those operating the smaller yachts that for six or seven days the interest of the crew is held and there are enough new and relatively simple experiences to hold their attention, and in the case of the more complex structure of a 150-ft craft this probationary period lasts for 13 or 14 days before the youngsters begin to look for further challenges.

Naturally there are exceptions to these one and two week voyages, but these are nearly always when an additional interest is introduced, such as carrying out some survey duties, ecological studies, or in the case of a voyage in which a race or rally of similar sail training craft is

Steering a 77-ft yacht is quite a reponsible job.

incorporated. You can now see why, in the case of those ships providing professional courses, the voyage length is likely to be of two or three months' duration; the shakedown period is similar to that of the medium craft but when the need for fresh experiences arises they are there, and in fact they are the reason for the voyage rather than the general benefits of sail training which I have already tried to explain.

The areas in which the ship will have to operate must also be a factor in determining its parameters, be they short passages between ports in Northern Europe or long trans-ocean voyages encompassing extremes of temperature and weather. They might even be confined to sailing in inland waterways and lakes, such as several schemes based in Canada. The ship may need central heating or the addition of partial or even complete air-conditioning with the resultant addition of a considerable amount of machinery. The sail area and the rig of the vessel is also likely to be determined by the area of the world in which she will operate.

Finally the finances of the organization which will operate the vessel have to be considered and this I will do in some depth in Chapter 8. The money available to build the ship may determine its size and complexity and its size may also be controlled by the number of youngsters to be carried and hence the revenue accrued from voyage fees. However, more of that later.

Watch-keeping at sea in *Dar Mlodziezy*.

On harbour watch aboard
Sedov.

So, I have not answered the question 'What is the ideal vessel?' All
I have done is to present a number of factors, often conflicting ones.
However, I will now try to give an answer or, rather, three answers
with a number of modifications. I have been fortunate enough to go
on board a large number of sail training ships belonging to a great
many countries and to study the way their organizations carry out
their tasks of training and I find it a most interesting fact that despite
the distances between countries and the fact that, in many cases, the
organizations did not realize that there were others in different parts
of the world carrying out precisely the same tasks as themselves,
they have so often reached the same set of compromises that I have
outlined in the above arguments.

When it comes to the rig there is much controversy. First let us
consider the relative merits of fore and aft rig as against square rig. I
believe there is little doubt that square rig is a far better training
medium, but gives bad performance when it comes to going to
windward — a direction which seems all too prevalent in most areas.
One great advantage is that of having to work aloft on the yards. At
first this is a great challenge to the youngsters; it looks and appears
extremely dangerous and much fear has to be overcome even to get
out to the ends of the yards, let alone carry out any work up there.
Statistics have proved otherwise, however, and after the first few times
clambering up and out, it becomes virtually second nature, but

continues to leave a feeling of pride. I love the story told to me by one man who had become a devotee of sail training through having sent his daughter away on a two-week voyage. He went down to the harbour to collect her at the end of the trip and he told me that to his horror as he arrived he saw her climbing aloft to re-stow one of the squaresails. The daughter he had sent away would never have done anything like that; she didn't say anything but her look plainly said:

'Play it cool, Dad.'

He told me that when she got home she did not say much at first about the voyage, but it was apparent that she had gained a very great deal from it and later on she talked with great pride about her part in it.

Not only is going aloft a challenge, but also the stowing of the sails can only be done by a number of the crew working together. It is a very uncontrived form of teamwork, as is the co-ordination required when tending the running rigging to set or hand a squaresail. Sheets, clewlines and buntlines must all be operated correctly to achieve the manoeuvre, and many evolutions can be satisfactorily carried out using squaresails which cannot be done so safely with fore and aft rig. I believe the thing which finally 'sold' square rig to me was on a day which I was invited to spend in the small Sea Cadet Corps brig

Preparing the ship for sailing — *Iskra* of the Polish Navy.

Royalist. I was able to compare the jobs being done by the crew with those that would have to be carried out on the large fore and aft rigged schooners or smaller ketches. In some cases they were very similar but there were many differences and one outstanding one was the fact that each and every trainee could be usefully employed at times. On a schooner or ketch, once the sails have been lowered it does not take very long to put a stow on them and after that many of the trainees are just standing around for quite a time with nothing to do waiting for the docking. There are very few jobs other than helping the permanent crew with the mooring lines or tending the fenders. In the square-rigger it is easier to keep sail on her for just a bit longer and then when the squaresails are clewed up, up go the youngsters to put a harbour stow on them; they are working aloft and are out of the way of the few who have to remain on deck for the lines and fenders. In short there is a mass of work for the whole ship's company to do, so no one has to stand around feeling 'spare'. So the brig with her two masts and, say, six squaresails is a good answer for the smaller vessel, as is the brigantine with two masts, square-

Getting ready to make sail on board *Sagres*.

The Island Cruising Club's *Hoshi*.

rigged on one. For the slightly larger ship the rigs of barquentine or barque are good; three masts which allow the sails to be of reasonable size and therefore not too heavy and difficult for young bodies to handle. As I have said, the main disadvantage is the poor windward performance of such rigs for although great speed and sailing performance are not an important factor in a sail training ship, the ability to reach different ports in a reasonable period of time is necessary if the balance of the voyage is to be efficient.

When it comes to fore and aft rig, the choice is a wide one. Firstly there is the division between Gaff rig and Bermudian. Gaff rig has one main advantage and that is the opportunity for teamwork since it needs two halliards (the ropes which haul a sail and its gear up the mast) in order to set it. These are the throat and peak halliards and if you pull on the former without, at the same time, pulling on the latter then the large and heavy gaff ends up emulating the broken wing of a bird; most un-nautical and liable to break something.

It reminds me of a story, someone else's story so I hope he will forgive me if I use it to illustrate a point. This well-known yachting editor ran a beautiful gaff-rigged schooner in the years after the war and sailed with charter crews. The ones he liked best were those who did not know the yacht well and would listen to his methods of how to handle the sails, so his heart sank when on starting to tell one crew from Yorkshire how to set the main he was brusquely interrupted:

'We've got us own method,' he was peremptorily told.

Ah well, he thought, I'd better let them get on with it, and as the yacht motored clear of the harbour in the dusk, he ordered the main to be set. Up it went and to his surprise there were no snags.

'Set the Headsails!' Again, not a hitch and so — 'Set the Foresail!' Up went the forward part of the sail, the throat halliard being heaved with a will, the end of the gaff did not stir and the sail began to have the look of a bird's broken wing and very soon there was going to be some damage.

'Stop!' roared the skipper 'Where's the peak halliard!'
'You can't 'ave peak 'alliard,' came a voice from forward. "E's in t' toilet.'

However, when the team is working well, good co-ordination produces good sail drills. There is also an opportunity for topsails, with their attendant sheets and possibly a vang or two, all good for making sure a watch has to co-ordinate its actions to achieve any result at all. Sadly, although with a better performance to windward than an equivalent size of square-rigger, the gaff rig loses out to Bermudian when trying to sail to windward.

In the case of the smaller craft of 40 to 75 ft, there is little doubt that the most versatile rig is that of the ketch, whether gaff or Bermudian-rigged. It is not as efficient as the single-masted sloop or cutter, but in modern vessels this margin is quite small and in addition there are a number of other advantages. The individual sails can be smaller if they are shared between two masts and provided that the design is right the great advantage is that the mainsail can be stowed and the yacht sailed in rough weather under mizzen plus one or two headsails. Usually it is good training and good practice to put reefs in the main, but there are times with a weak and perhaps seasick crew when the afterguard can whip the main down, put a rough sea-stow on it, and sail on confidently with the boat much more upright and under good control and with no worries. The mizzen mast also provides the wherewithal to set a fifth sail, the mizzen staysail.

In the case of craft larger than about 75 ft, many organizations have found that the two-masted schooner is a good choice. As the length of the hull increases so does the size of each of the sails and therefore at about 100 ft, it is probably necessary to have a third mast in order that the sails can be handled by the young crews. It is an interesting fact that the third mast takes a heavy toll on the ship's sailing ability, and I believe that this is because the mast itself and its associated rigging causes a great deal of extra windage which thus hinders the performance. There is little doubt that if it is practical to handle the sails of a two-mast rig, this is preferable. For ships of over about 80 ft the addition of one or more yards may be possible with only a relatively small loss of sailing ability and with all the advantages already discussed. This immediately leads to the possibility of a staysail schooner or a barquentine, both rigs allowing relatively small and easily handled sails.

To summarize the rig, for the smaller sail trainer I would

recommend a ketch rig, for the medium-sized vessel a three-masted barquentine or schooner rig, and for the large ship there is a good choice, perhaps three-masted barque or full-rigged ship where the difference in performance will be marginal and expense is probably a more important factor.

Next I will consider the layout below decks. The main factors that have to be considered are accommodation for the afterguard and for the crew, machinery space, cooking area, navigation, lavatories and washing areas and storage. It has been found to be important that, if possible, even on the smallest training ship the afterguard should be able to isolate themselves at times from the young crew. Both the adults and the youngsters appreciate this, since neither group necessarily wants the other's company all of the time, each welcomes the opportunity to talk about the other in complimentary terms — or otherwise! On the other hand, it is important that as many of the ship's company as possible can sit down together for meals and also for briefings or instruction from time to time. Bearing in mind these two factors, the layout of a small yacht usually only allows for a four berth cabin aft, possibly with a water-tight bulkhead at its forward end but at least a bulkhead and door separating it from the rest of the boat.

It is probably best then to have a galley on one side of the ship with a navigating area opposite it, to allow these two functions to be carried out near to the centre of the vessel and in a place where there is the least pitching movement. Both these areas must be of reasonable size, because sail training craft tend to have larger crews than private yachts of similar size and therefore meals for relatively large numbers have to be cooked by the unskilled under the supervision of the slightly more skilled. While the navigator is plying his magic art, it is desirable that there should be room enough for two or more of the trainees to watch and to help him if they show an interest.

Forward of these two areas the crew accommodation can start, either in one open-plan area with two or three levels of bunks with associated kit lockers and with a table or tables in the centre. The best place for the heads (lavatories) and washing area is right forward in the bows; this is where the pitching will be worst and this area is probably best utitlized for these functions rather than try to sleep or cook there. On anything but the smallest yacht it should be possible to isolate the heads area by means of a reasonably solid bulkhead and door, whereas in a small yacht it is probably only possible to have plywood bulkheads. Plenty of light down below and good ventilation even when the fore-hatch has to be battened down in heavy weather conditions is essential for reasonable living conditions. The machinery on a relatively small yacht can easily be located under or half under the deck.

On a medium-sized vessel, the above conventions are usually observed so that the layout is not dissimilar, although machinery is

Georg Stage under full sail.

more complicated, takes up much more room and is usually located between the accommodation for the afterguard and that of the trainees. It is then the usual practice both for safety and convenience to have water-tight bulkheads at the forward and aft ends of this space. It is likely that this size of vessel will have at least one deck-house and it is kind to the cook as well as those who have to live below decks if the galley can be one of the main areas located in it.

One use of a deck-house which I have admired on several newly-built training areas is a structure containing only seats and a table; on one such ship it is called 'The Bus Shelter'. It is most useful for a number of functions; in poor weather people can carry their meals there and eat them in sheltered conditions whilst they are virtually on deck rather than battened down below; it can be used as a teaching or briefing area and the stand-by watch or part of the duty watch can lurk there in safety and shelter when not needed for sail changes, sheet trimming and so on. I have seen such a deck-house on craft varying between 70 and 150 ft length. One mistake that has been made in several medium-sized ships is to crowd too much into the navigation area or chart-room. It is important to have a quite separate area from which to control the ship to that used by the afterguard for their eating and relaxing area.

It is virtually impossible to run a sail training ship without auxiliary power because, apart from safety reasons, it is an essential require-

ment of modern life that schedules are maintained, and if the ship is
due to arrive at a certain port at a certain time then there is no time
to wait for a fair wind or a favourable tide. The merchant schooners
of the early part of this century were able to do just that and they
became experts at working tides, but they had to be prepared to
remain at anchor if the wind was too light, too strong or too
unfavourable in direction. Once again I will consider the sail training
yacht and the medium-sized ship separately. The yacht is likely to
present no problem. For some years now, relatively light and powerful
diesel engines have been available which take up virtually half the
space of the earlier models and these can be located under the
cockpit, under a semi-raised deck-house or even under the cabin
floor. They can be fitted with one or two powerful alternators which
in turn can charge an engine starter battery and a domestic battery at
the same time at a healthy 40 or 50 amps if required. For this
reason, on the smallest yacht it is probably unnecessary to have a
separate generator, although many of the 70-footers do have one.
Because schedules have to be met, the amount of power available
from the auxiliary engine should be generous, of the order of 60 bhp
for a 40-footer and 100 bhp for the 75-footer. These sizes of craft do
not really need a powered anchor winch, but if such assistance is
thought to be necessary a hydraulic pump can be run off the engine
to provide power for a windlass. It is sensible to take a drive for a
general service pump from the engine, too, which can then be used
as a combined fire pump and bilge pump determined by the position
of a series of cocks.

The 100 to 150 ft ships need an altogether more sophisticated
machinery fit. Two engines are desirable for reliability and each
should be of the order of 200 bhp for a 150-footer. The STA
Schooners have two 135 bhp engines and the combined power is
only just adequate. What this means is that should they have to
motor against a force 8 wind, because of the windage of the two
yards and the masts and rigging, they have to tack up wind to achieve
satisfactory progress. The *Captain Scott*, only slightly bigger and with
four rather than two yards, had two 230 bhp engines and she could
motor straight into a force 8 and achieve a safe speed of about four
knots.

The electrical system on such vessels is a matter of choice. Until
about 1980 most ships of this size were fitted with a large bank of
batteries, in some cases working at 115 volts and in a few cases on
24 or 48 volts. The theory was that by running all the domestic
electrics from a battery, quite a large proportion of the day could be
passed without the unpleasant roar of a generator running. The vessel
was a sailing vessel and could get on with sailing without the constant
noise of an engine. Incidentally it may surprise people to realize that
very often the trainees think that the ship is motoring when in fact
the main engines are off and it is only the noisy generator which is
running. In practice once the batteries are past their first flush of

youth — and that often seems to be quite shortly after they are installed — it will be found necessary to charge for at least eight out of the 24 hours of the day, and furthermore the batteries are very heavy and require quite a lot of cosseting! Modern ships often have a 115V or 240V AC electrical system which is powered from one of two alternators auxiliary to the main engines and mounted in well sound-proofed 'boxes'. One of them has to be run constantly throughout the time that the ship is in commission unless shore power is available and at times when a heavy electrical load is required, such as when operating electrically powered anchor windlass and capstan. Then both may run in parallel or at other times they are run alternately. With good design and great care taken over their sound-proofing the resultant noise can turn out to be little more than the general sound of fans and other machinery which would be running anyway.

These larger vessels do require some power assistance in the bows for raising the anchor and additionally at the aft end of the ship for hauling in mooring ropes, and these can be powered by hydraulics or electricity according to taste. I have worked with both forms and cannot say that one is outstandingly better than the other. Again the larger vessel will also have a much more complicated system of plumbing, probably with septic tanks for basins, sinks and showers, and a complicated system of bilge pumping. All these systems will have to be designed professionally and there are many existing examples of large sailing ships from which ideas can be gleaned. There is one factor which often suffers from bad planning and that is that most marine designers and builders are unused to dealing with large sailing ships rather than motor ships and the former have one characteristic which is very unusual — they heel over! What is more they heel over to one side and stay over, sometimes for days at a time; they may heel to twenty degrees and then role between thirty and ten degrees. Now anyone who has been in a sailing ship knows this and accepts it as a matter of course, but what the designer, the builder and even the sailor may not realize is that the plumbing has to be designed to cope with the phenomenon. A septic tank sited below the basins which it serves and with only a fifteen degree fall is going to discharge itself happily into those basins if the ship heels to twenty degrees! If you try to solve the problem by fitting a non-return valve into the system it will stop the flooding back but the basin still will not empty. Basins are one matter, bilge pumping systems are far more important and so are engine cooling and lubricating systems.

Another calculation which I have seen go wrong with the planning of at least three newly-constructed sail training ships is the size and weight of the anchor gear. A large sailing vessel has an enormous amount of windage, particularly if it has two or more yards and with ratlines on some of the shrouds, and this is an important factor when the ship is at anchor, for that windage increases the vessel's chances of dragging. I believe that the figures for the weights of anchors and their cable sizes as laid down in Lloyds' specifications are too low for practical purposes. The penalty of getting too light a size for the anchors and too light a cable for the anchors, can be a severe one; in one case it was found that a heavier chain was needed and this meant a change of gypsy on the anchor windlass and it was subsequently found that because of all this heavier gear the motor on the windlass was not man enough to handle it and in the nearly-new ship a generator had to be removed and replaced by one of greater power.

In all sizes of ship the capacity of fresh water and fuel which is carried must depend very much on the general nature of the ship's operation and also on any 'one off' operation she may have to carry out. In the case of the yacht, the conventional capacities will probably be acceptable; a crew of twelve young trainees will almost certainly use less water than the private owner's family of four! a 70 ft ship probably needs about 3 tons (600 gallons) of fresh water, to avoid having to top up more than once in the middle of a seven day course, while a fuel capacity of 100 gallons will probably be right. The 150-footer would not be overdoing things if she had a fresh water capacity of 30 tons and able to carry 8 or 10 tons of fuel, particularly if that fuel is to power the generator(s), galley stove and domestic heating system in addition to the main engine. It should also be remembered that fresh water distillation plants use a great deal of fuel; the captain of *Eagle* told me that when they are producing fresh water they use fuel at about the same rate as when they run their main engine.

If I was going to have a new sail training ship built, I would make a point of trying to get permission to study the plans of and get aboard to have a close look at as many of the craft operated by well-established sail training schemes as possible. Many of them have now been in existence long enough to have started with second-hand vessels not designed specifically for their purpose, then progressed to custom built second generation ships in which quite a lot of things still turned out to be wrong, and thence to the third generation from which they have learnt the lessons of the previous two and have then got everything pretty well right. Most organizations would be happy to share their experience and knowledge to help someone start a new scheme or improve on their existing one.

The Bells of Rhymney

A sad little song which sets out to copy the church bells of the Welsh valley towns. It has a very difficult but extremely effective guitar accompaniment which imitates the bells.

'Oh what will you give me?' say the sad bells of Rhymney.
'Is there hope for the future?' say the brown bells of Merthyr.
'Who made the mine owner?' say the black bells of Rhonda,
'And who robbed the miners?' say the grim bells of Blaina.

'They will plunder willy-nilly,' say the bells of Caerphilly,
'They have fangs, they have teeth,' shout the loud bells of Neath.
'Even God is uneasy,' say the moist bells of Swansea,
'And what will you give me?' say the sad bells of Rhymney.

'Oh the vandal's in court,' say the bells of Newport,
'All will be well, if, if, if, if, if,' say the green bells of Cardiff,
'Why so worried, sisters, why?', sang the silver bells of Wye,
'And what will you give me?' say the sad bells of Rhymney.

Words by Idris Davies and music by Pete Seager.

Chapter 7
The Ideal Crew

Throughout this book I have made mention of various terms to describe the people on board a sail training vessel. I am now going to mention various attributes and criteria which affect the master, captain or skipper, the mates and other deck officers (afterguard), the petty officers, the trainee leaders (watch leaders etc), and the trainee crew.

In any sea-going vessel the captain has to be the most important character on board in order for the ship to be run safely and successfully. 'Master under God!' was an old-fashioned description of the captain. He must have an unquestionable knowledge and practical ability of seamanship such that, whatever the conditions of wind and weather, those organizers remaining ashore can feel secure in the knowledge that whatever punishment their ship may be enduring, the captain is coping with it in the most professional and successful manner possible. He must also have a strong personality and an excellent mastery of the art of leadership. In addition, he must have the ability to get the very best out of a crew of young people and ensure that by his planning and execution of the voyage, they get the most out of their time on board. Throughout this description of captain and crew, it is extremely important to remember that whereas the captain, the mate or anyone else on board a Navy or Merchant Navy ship may have great skill at seamanship, cargo handling and other technicalities and be in every way a splendid operator in their ship, they do not automatically have the two extra qualifications to work in a sail training craft, namely a deep knowledge of handling a vessel propelled by sails and a strong ability to work with youngsters. Furthermore they have the full backing of their service or company behind them. Let me hasten to say that this works the other way round, too; a paragon of sail training, born sailor and brilliant youth leader would almost certainly be unable to act as chief officer or master of a super-tanker or of any other specialized ship.

When the British sail training schemes were starting in the early '60s, Commander Walter Scott used to say:

'There are only about a thousand yachtsmen in Britain who are able

Owner, Skipper and Carpenter — Heinrich Woermann of *Olifant*.

to skipper a 75 ft yacht and, of those probably only half can at the same time get the very best out of a crew of youngsters. I'm looking for 50 of them.'

Happily the number of suitably-qualified yachtsmen is now probably much higher than a thousand because there are many more opportunities to sail in yachts of 75 ft and over. The number has also increased due to the success of a number of sail training schemes and the encouragement they give to their leaders to increase their knowledge and sailing ability. What remains absolutely vital is the combination of the ability to skipper safely with that of leadership. In the case of the larger ships, such as *Sir Winston Churchill*, the seamanship criterion is not that of being a highly competent yachtsman but rather of being highly competent as the master of a small ship, but still with the same sailing and leadership endorsements.

Let us assume, then, that our captain is an expert sailor and has all the attributes of leadership that we could wish. If he has been provided with a reasonable back-up of watch keepers and more junior leaders, then while things are running smoothly, his is a 'stand back' role. His main preoccupation should be voyage planning and in this he is helped by the fact that virtually all the organizations tell him which is to be his starting port and the date and the time to be at the final port of the voyage, and then leave what happens in between to the master. There is always a strong temptation for the shore organizers to pop in one or more engagements in between the start and the end of the cruise, but they should strongly resist doing so. If the master is permitted to select his own course of action between the start and the end, he is then likely to be in a position to make the very best use of the weather and geographical conditions which exist. Any commitment in the middle of the voyage will immediately introduce a second deadline and mean that the plans will then become considerably less flexible.

There are five main factors when considering voyage plans:

The time available to travel from the start port to the final port;
The weather conditions at the start of the voyage;
The type of crew embarked and their likely ability;
The likely future weather development;
The state of the crew as induced by conditions met so far.

The first three of these factors are set for a particular voyage and can be used immediately to formulate the basic outline of the passage. The ship may be leaving from and end at the same port or the two ports may be some considerable distance apart and in either case a rough plan has to be made to provide an interesting mixture of time at sea and time in port. If they can be determined, the likely wind directions during the period of the voyage should be borne in mind because although some windward work is almost inevitable it is always more pleasant to sail off the wind, and if possible ports should be chosen accordingly. The weather at the start of the voyage is, of course, a set fact. In the very worst case it may dictate a delayed start, always a very difficult situation for any captain because the more inexperienced the crew the more unlikely they are to appreciate that what may seem an exciting breeze in harbour is in fact a rather horrid gale just the other side of the sea wall. I have just read a report where the Master of a sail training schooner, while walking along a sea wall to check out conditions, caught a small Pekinese dog — this confirmed his decision not to sail!

At this early stage of their time on board, the young crew will be raring to go and if sailing has to be delayed then much thought should be put into how to keep the youngsters busy in as uncontrived a fashion as possible. A flat calm at the start of the voyage can also be difficult because it is then very hard to give any impression of what ship manoeuvres are really like. It can sometimes lead to dangerous situations when the wind does eventually blow if the crew has become blasé about the gear.

However, let us assume that all is well with the weather and after a minimum of training alongside or at the mooring, we are under way. This training is then continued by carrying out some tacks and gybes and any other manoeuvres deemed sensible before settling down for the first passage. It is at this point that the last two factors should be taken into account. Weather has to be a predominant factor in the operation of a sailing ship and all masters should take every opportunity to appraise themselves of forecasts for the area in which they are sailing. In British waters, the obtaining of the BBC shipping forecast should be a ritual of as great an importance as a mealtime. When I was in the *Captain Scott*, it was the duty of one of the trainee crew, the navigator's yeoman, to listen to and write down the shipping forecast. Of course in the early part of the voyage this was done in conjunction with the officer of the watch, but once they had got the hang of it they took it down on their own. On occasions they forgot all about it and then, some ten minutes after the forecast time, a woebegone navigator's yeoman would report to me having been sent by the captain. A glance at my watch and I did not need to ask what his misdemeanour had been.

'You know what to do?'

Up the rigging he would climb to the very top of the foremast.

'Have you anything to tell us?', I would shout up to him.
'MY NAME IS SMITH,' he would roar. 'I'VE JUST MISSED THE WEATHER FORECAST!'

This announcement from aloft would produce a muffled cheer from below and I am happy to say that most navigator's yeomen only missed one forecast.

Incidentally before you reach for your pen to dash off a letter to a national authority for the prevention of cruelty to trainees, I think I should reassure you that I knew perfectly well those youngsters who were scared of going aloft or who could not take such ribaldry; in which case I would either forget to send them up or find something else for them to do, such as an extra duty in the galley, which I knew perfectly well would start with a piece of cherry cake and a sympathetic word from Margo the cook. I should also add that the whole thing was done in a great spirit of humour and occasionally I came off the worst, such as the time when sailing with an adult crew, when the gentleman invited to say what he had to tell us, roared from his eyrie:

'OYEZ! OYEZ! OYEZ! MY NAME IS JONES . . .'

Back to the likely weather development. This, coupled with the state of the crew, will determine at what stage to put into port and how long to stay there before setting out on the next leg of the voyage. This crew state is constantly in the Captain's mind; it is no good exhausting the youngsters, which can be easily done, as they are quite unused to the broken sleep pattern, the ship's routine and the large doses of fresh sea air. On the other hand, if conditions are very easy and there is not much heaving and hauling to be done, they may be having too easy a time and need some extra activity. Throughout the voyage the master has to make this continuous assessment of his crew's condition and state.

Most organizations have a number of suggestions as to what can be done with a young crew if the ship is gale-bound in port. Very often the captain is authorized to hire a coach in order to visit some place of local interest or he will get his officers to organize the crew in some sporting or cultural activity. Apart from that there is always a

Above *Jolie Brize* owned by Exeter Maritime Museum and sailed in the summer by pupils from Dauntsey's School. A very famous yacht with a racing and sail training history.

Left *Dusmarie* — small but stalwart.

Far left *Aztec Lady* who sailed to Australia in 1987.

Left Steering demands a lot of concentration.

Below Tying down a reef needs teamwork.

never-ending supply of jobs such as cleaning and maintenance to be done in the ship. It is when periods of calm are experienced in mid-voyage that planning may be difficult, particularly if the previous passages have been blessed with some exciting strong wind sailing, and it is then that the captain really has to think out how to keep his crew interested and yet not by too contrived a situation. As an example I remember being in a sail training yacht moored at Cowes on the Isle of Wight and lying in my bunk in just such a predicament, wondering what I could do to keep eight delinquent boys busy on a day when there was thick fog in the Solent and not a breath of wind. While still half awake, I dreamed up a happy little scheme.

Secret plans had been stolen from a nearby factory by two spies from different countries. The spies had gone into town, hidden a secret message to reveal their whereabouts, then gone up to Newport (six miles up the river Medina). The first spy to be found by his watch and brought back to the yacht would be afforded passage back to his own country with the plans. Great: the two spies are the two watch officers, with two rubber dinghies available which can each carry four people, that's four youngsters up to Newport. Then when they meet up with their 'spy', still only four in the dinghy, there will be a need for a water-borne party together with a land party from each watch — better and better!

I prepared to confront the eight lads with this spendid '*Boy's Own*' epic but then had grave second thoughts; I'd never get away with it. Spies, secret plans, hidden notes — not in the '80s for heaven's sake! But what else was there to do with them?

'Right, listen lads . . .'

As my story unfolded, I could sense an air of excitement building up, soon they couldn't wait to start. Each watch of four rowed furiously across to the landing place and rushed into Cowes searching for their hidden message. I got on with some maintenance and hoped. Four hours later I looked up, two rubber dinghies racing neck and neck, (or is it prow and prow?) towards the yacht — a dead heat; a look ashore and there were the land members of the watches escorting their 'spies'. Both watches arrived on board, quite breathless, at the same moment, a great scheme. And what was the talk all about when they got back to the community home at the end of the cruise? Sailing? Not a bit of it. Secret plans, spies and a race back to base . . . Ah well, perhaps things don't change so much after all.

The captain must have a strong personality. His position as 'Master under God' means that everyone else on board is half watching him and taking their lead and their tempo from him; he must drive when everyone has become lethargic, sympathize when life is difficult, adjudicate if a grievance is expressed, make a decision when one is called for. He is alone and his reaction to a situation may, in the most serious cases such as a man overboard, mean the difference between

Far left Climbing out over the futtock shrouds is very scaring the first time you have to do it.

life and death, or in a less dramatic situation, between a happy crew member or a disgruntled one. Has it struck you yet how very few sanctions he has available to him? What can he do if a youngster refuses an order? Keel-hauling is discouraged — it would not look too good in the newspapers! Physical punishment is most decidedly out, since if shore establishments are not permitted to use it then neither can sail training schemes. Probably the most serious situation is the outright refusal to obey an order and because of this one gets used to quickly thinking ahead to make sure that whatever orders may be given, such a situation will not arise.

Happily one of the joys of this form of training is that virtually all tasks that have to be done can clearly be seen to be uncontrived. The novice can easily see the necessity for any task he or she is given to do and the effect on himself, the others of his watch or the ship if the job is not carried out quickly and efficiently, and therefore he usually gets on with it without question. However, the 'Why me?' situation can often occur and leadership by example becomes vitally important. If confronted by a blank refusal to carry out an order, I believe that each captain must resolve the situation in his own way, depending upon the circumstances and the individual concerned. Perhaps you will allow me two examples, both of which truly happened to me. I dealt with both in a completely different manner, and in both cases I managed to break the impasse.

The first case involved a soldier, one of a crew which I had brought down from the regiment in which I was serving at the time to sail in one of the big sail training yachts as an adventure training exercise. We were in mid-channel, beating into a rather nasty short sea and the yacht had made quite a lot of water, you could hear it sloshing around in the deep bilges and a glance under the floorboards confirmed this, revealing a black, oily, swimming pool of heaving bilge-water. We really should have pumped much earlier. Anyway, I asked the watch officer to get one of the lads to pump. Off went one to the pump and pumped away with a will, soon he was relieved by another, but after his regulation 200 strokes there came a fracas. Number three refused, he was tired, feeling seasick, didn't want to be where he was and wasn't going to pump — no way. I listened to the confrontation between the young solider and his officer. Now this was doubly serious; a crew member refusing an order was a problem that could not be ignored, but a soldier disobeying an order from his officer was even worse.

'Come here,' I ordered, and led the way down below. 'Now, did I hear you being told to pump the bilges?'
'It ain't my turn. Anyway, I'm cold and I'm sick and I wish I 'adn't come on this bloomin' boat. Why should I pump it?' he asked.

I raised the board again, the boat lurched over a wave and the oily water sloshed noisily across.

'Because if you don't, we'll sink!' I replied.

He was gone and then I heard rapid sounds of pumping. It was unfair, it was cruel and it has caused me a lot of thought since. But it broke the spell and anyway he was a rough, tough soldier and that was not going to frighten him for the rest of his life.

The build up to the other case was very similar. This time the pumpee had just come off watch and had been asked to pump the bilges, instead he had shot into his bunk and was lying there, hull down and refusing. This time it was a quite different sort of lad, quiet and nervous, and I knew that he had come on board from a community home. Once again I listened as the battle of wits progressed, the order, the refusal, the appeal for reason. I lay 'asleep' in the deck-house, realizing that an appeal was very soon going to be made to the highest authority available — me! What is more I knew that I too was quite likely not going to be able to make him pump either. I got up, descended into the saloon and started working the pump, loudly and ostentatiously. After about 400 strokes (that takes quite a time), I said in a conversational tone and as if I had not heard any of the foregoing dialogue:

'Bob, can you come and take over from me? I want to go up and check our position.'

It worked. I am sure that the lad realized the whole subterfuge, but it was a way to break the impasse between his watch officer and himself which had been needed, and he took it. I'm glad he did, because once an order has been refused and no action is taken, that lad will almost certainly be a problem for the rest of the voyage. Incidentally, we do not spend our entire time at sea pumping; those just seemed to be good contrasting examples.

Some sanctions can be imposed and some are very obvious. For example, a time limit is always announced to the crew before shore leave is granted. By that I mean a time by which all must be back on board and a late returner might well find himself as a punishment doing harbour watch during the next period of shore leave. Ah, but what happens on the last evening with the crew due to leave next day? Well, I believe that if you have not managed to put across the discipline message by that time, either the voyage length is too short or you have failed your crew.

The captain's example is vitally important, although everyone's personality is different and each captain will behave in a different way, his demeanour matching his personality. Personally I am a great believer in creating an air of expectation. I always like the report, probably apocryphal, by a commanding officer of one of his juniors:

'His men will follow this officer to the utmost ends of the earth — if only out of a sense of curiosity to see what he will do next.'

I am reminded of a girls' voyage in one of the STA schooners. Once again, conditions were extremely uncomfortable with a full gale blowing, and the ship although well snugged down, jumping about a lot in the seaway. It had been a long, dark night and because of the conditions the captain had spent most of it either on the bridge or dozing in a corner of the chartroom. The watches changed and the old watch went down into the half-deck (the trainees' messdeck and not always a happy sight in a seaway). Suddenly one of the girls became slightly hysterical, demanding to see the captain. Her watch leader could not calm her and she shot up into the chartroom where the ship's officers live:

'I've got to see the captain,' she cried.
'But he's only just turned in,' came the answer. 'He's been up all night. Is it really important enough to disturb him so soon?'
'He's gone to bed?' queried the girl.
'Yes.'
'Oh well, if he's gone to bed it can't be as bad as I thought it was,' she said and, vastly reassured, she went quietly back down to the halfdeck and so to sleep herself.

There is one modern development which eases the captains' problems to a very great extent, particularly the captains — or skippers — of the smaller craft, and that is knowing where he is! Now that may sound rather an odd statement; surely captains have always known where they are? Not so. In the days prior to the arrival of modern, sophisticated electronic navigational aids, after a passage of, say, a hundred miles involving a series of strong cross tides and in bad visibility — such as a voyage from the Solent to Le Havre — the navigation would have been done by dead reckoning and an estimated position would have been obtained by plotting on the chart the courses steered and marking off the distance sailed. Now these courses would have been obtained from what the novice helmsman declared that he had steered, using a magnetic compass which itself is prey to many errors, some known and some unknown. The distance would have been determined by the ship's log, an instrument of varying accuracy. The tidal set would have been calculated from tables in the doubtful knowledge that the tables can only allow for average conditions. If that passage was made in conditions of having to beat into high winds and heavy seas, the accuracy of the position at the end would be in even greater doubt.

Electronic navigational aids have been available since the 1940s, such devices as Consol which was developed from the bombing aircrafts' systems, radio direction finding, radar and parabolic navigational systems such as Decca and Loran. The problem was that the equipment on board ships was large, heavy and consumed immoderate quantities of electricity. I well remember the Mark 5 Decca which whirred away to itself in a large steel wardrobe, had a very large display mounted over the chart table and needed about 30 amps of power the entire time it was operating. Radar equipment was much larger, used even more power and did not give particularly good account of itself in small vessels. The small vessels themselves were a most unhappy environment for the electronic circuits of the time, consisting as they did of large numbers of valves and other components which did not take kindly to being bumped about in a salt-laden atmosphere.

Then came the transistor to be followed very shortly by many thousands of transistors all sealed inside a small 'chip'. Now the chips are physically far less vulnerable to the environment in which they find themselves working, can do the work of drawers and cupboards full of the old-fashioned circuitry and, of the greatest importance, they need very small amounts of power. The current state of the art for equipment using the the Decca system has no wardrobe, no gigantic display and no mammoth hunger for power. I remember the new equipment arriving for the three London Sailing Project boats in early 1986. I was shown the units and said,

'That's just the display unit, there must be another box that connects to it, probably goes under the chart table.'

A search revealed nothing else, just the small flat unit that had originally emerged from the box.

'This must be it,' said the fleet officer.
'Can't be,' I said because after all I was interested in and had quite a working knowledge of electronics.

It *was* it. There was nothing else. All the receivers, computer circuits and display were in the one small flat unit; small enough to be popped into a brief case and taken home at the end of the voyage for re-programming ready for the next one. The facilities which were available other than just the raw position in latitude and longitude are hardly credible, even to those with a working knowledge of electronics, and its accuracy is also remarkable. The yacht radars now available are similarly startling in regard to size, power consumption and efficiency. Add to all this a price which has plummeted from tens of thousands of pounds in the 1950s to hundreds currently and you will realize that nearly all sail training ships have both radar and either an hyperbolic navigation device or a satellite navigator fitted.

So now we know where we are, but this has given rise to some controversy, namely the 'What if the fuse blows?' syndrome. That same marine environment which upset the earlier equipment is still present and even modern electronics are susceptible to some degree. The new equipment does not need much power, but it must have some supply, so what if the batteries go flat? Perhaps we should not allow the young watch officer to use the equipment, perhaps we should hide it in the skipper's cabin or fit it with an 'ignition key' so that only the privileged can switch it on.

I fully realize the importance of ensuring that the modern generation of sail training officers learns the old-fashioned methods of navigation so that should all the modern aids fail, they can still fall back on the old methods and make safe land-falls. However, I believe that they are aware of this need to learn, but also that they need to understand and appreciate the modern aids as well. I have found that those to whom all these devices are not new and awesome but a fact of life, can cope with the use of the electronics while at the same time switching off the displays and running up an estimated position as if the equipment were not working. It is then most interesting to compare the chart work position with where the electronics believe you to be.

From an overall point of view, it is immensely encouraging to know where you are, to be able to come to anchor in safety, to manoeuvre in bad visibility if that has become necessary. It all removes a very large area of worry from the mind of the captain and his officers; it allows more time to ensure that the young crew get as much out of the voyage as possible.

The chief officer or mate has almost as important a role as his captain. He should be a deputy for him and just as an airliner has two pilots so too should a sailing ship have two people on board able to handle the ship. At least the mate should be able to get her into port or into a safe situation such as an anchorage if his captain should become incapacitated. It may sound very obvious but he should also know the captain's overall plan, the ship's position and where she is bound. Fortunately it is extremely rare for this second pilot situation to be needed. In everyday life it is the mate's task to present his captain with a ship which works, which enables the captain to go when and where he wants.

Every ship must have a routine and it is extremely important that this routine is maintained throughout the 24 hour period. I have already described the watch system in some detail. Dovetailed into this must be the meal times, cleaning, maintenance, navigation and all the procedures for the ship to be conducted safely at sea. The routine must also allow for time spent alongside in harbour, at a mooring buoy or at anchor (a typical medium-sized ship's routine is given in Chapter 3). It must make provision for the right number of people to be available to set sail, to hand sail, to tack or gybe, to shorten sail or just to sail. Drills have to be worked up and the right number of crew available for coming alongside a dock, anchoring, sending a boat away, catching fire and extinguishing same, action to be taken in the event of collision and so on. In a new ship it is usually the mate's responsibility to organize all these aspects and once the ship is running, to make sure that everyone on board knows where they are supposed to be, whatever evolution is taking place.

A good mate will monitor the ship's routine constantly and jump on anyone who does not do what they have to when they have to do it. As soon as one thing slips, for example a meal is late, then everything slips after it, the watch is late on deck, the washing up is delayed, so is the preparation of the next meal, and almost certainly the captain will have wanted the sails handed immediately after the end of the meal because he is going into port . . . A good mate will complement his captain, he will protect him, even from crew members who will not pump, he will help to elevate him on to a slightly raised pedestal. At the same time he can, if convenient, hide behind him:

'You know the Captain doesn't like that . . .'

The mate is also responsible to the captain for the state of maintenance of the ship, the amount that he does or that he oversees, depending upon the size of the ship, the number, if any, of assistants he has and the dictates of his organization. A mate worth his salt is almost certainly hoping to be a captain himself before too long and he should be able to anticipate what his captain needs and be putting it into action before it is required. For example, a ship about to enter harbour and moor alongside is going to need a headline, a sternline and two springs in addition to fenders. The mate has been told the estimated time of arrival, and anyway he can see the progress towards the port, so it should not be necessary for the captain to order the equipment to be brought up and laid out. The mate also has the responsibility of co-ordinating the hands when more than one watch is needed for an evolution. In this respect he can ensure that everyone gets a fair crack at all the jobs, the pleasant ones and the not so pleasant. On a medium-sized ship with, say, 55 people on board, a well-organized mate is kept constantly busy with the plans and he should quite frequently call together his watch officers and brief them as to exactly which tasks they are to do for the next evolutions to be carried out.

Ideally the captain and the mate should be opposites in temperament; a quiet, reserved captain needs a 'bucko' mate, while a noisy captain who likes to do quite a lot himself, needs a quiet, sympathetic mate. Two buccaneers or two over-scholarly types are a mistake. Quite often it becomes necessary to assume the role appropriate to the situation, I remember meeting the parents of one girl who had been a trainee on a voyage on an occasion when I had been the mate of one of the STA schooners.

'Mummy, Daddy,' she said on returning home, 'I've just suffered under the nastiest man I've ever met, that mate!' I insisted that it was all an act, saying that I honestly believed that the girls were expecting a rolling, swaggering, mean, nasty type of mate, so they got one, particularly as the captain I was sailing with was far too kind to them! What is difficult is when the time comes for the mate to be promoted to captain, when he probably has to play the whole thing differently. But thus it ever was, because Shem, Ham or Japheth must have eventually earned their Master's Certificates and taken over command! (That will show you how long I have been involved with sail training.)

In most schemes, as we have discovered, the captain is on board in a permanent capacity, and in the larger ships so too is the mate. Very often the watch-keeping officers are temporary, and this has great

stalwarts who paint the Forth Bridge. He is also a vital man when it comes to heavy work to be done on deck, such as reefing sails or, in the early part of the voyage, to work with the mate, both having eyes everywhere as sails are set for the first time. In a big manoeuvre such as a tack or a gybe, the mate will very often supervise one half of the deck while the bosun looks after the other half, watching and advising where necessary. One crafty bosun I knew always used to secure important ropes with a double back-hitch, a particular way of finishing off the securing of a rope to a pin and frowned upon in many ships because of the possibility of it jamming under load, particularly in the days when ropes were made of natural fibre. Sometimes he used a double back-hitch and on rare occasions a triple one; when asked why, he replied:

'Gives me time to get across the deck to 'em afore they goes and drops the boom on someone's 'ead!'

Next the chef. Need I tell you, gentle reader, more of the importance of the chef? But what of his job? Before the start of the voyage he must plan his menus and thus prepare his order list. When the stores arrive, in the pouring rain of course, he must check them and supervise their stowage so that items are reachable when needed but not prone to damage in a seaway — then he must cook. Try cooking in a kitchen that is tilted to 15° from the horizontal and then rolling from side to side as well; put a knife down on the table and then go and pick it up from the leeward scuppers. Put a roast in the oven and then realize after 40 minutes that the fire in your range was blown out by the down-draft from the mainsail — but how long ago? Try and crack 50 eggs into a frying pan with one hand while you fight to keep yourself standing steady with the other. Remember to prop up the leeward side of the baking dish with a brick to compensate for the ship's angle of heel — and change the brick over on hearing the order 'Ready About' prior to the ship tacking and then heeling the other way. Then smile and instruct your two 'galley rats' in the gentle art of washing up. Wake up at 0530 in the morning and immediately start thinking 'What shall we have for lunch today?' or, more likely, 'What will it be possible to cook for lunch today?' 'Tis not an easy life cooking three hot meals a day for 20, 30 or even 60 people. Sea cooks are a rare breed (and by no means are they all born out of wedlock!).

These three experts must also have the same double attributes as the captain and the mate in that they must not only be experts at their speciality but also expert at getting the best out of a crew of young people and helping them to make the most of their time on board. The young people are the reason for the ship's existence.

At one time I was very interested in the possibility of starting a 'Promotion Ladder' for people who became interested in sail training at an early age, had a job as, say, bosun in a 70-footer and were interested in pursuing a career in this specialized world. As an example, I felt that the youngster might work his way through watch leader perhaps to bosun in a medium-sized schooner, come back to the smaller boats as a watch officer and from there progress to mate. Then perhaps move to a job as a junior watch-keeper in the medium-sized ships and soon afterwards, back to the smaller boats as skipper. Then, with a wealth of experience behind him by now, he might eventually aspire to mate and then skipper of one of the bigger sail training ships. Sadly my idea did not work for two reasons, First the various organizations who had managed to find a really good young leader understandably did not wish to lose him or her to another sailing scheme. The other reason is that once you get to a certain size of ship, then the 'amateur' qualifications available through the Royal Yachting Association and Department of Transport Coastal Skipper and Yachtmaster schemes are not sufficient. Department of Transport Masters' Certificates of various grades become necessary and in order to be allowed to sit for these, a considerable amount of sea time in Department-recognized ships is required; most of the experience gained in the schemes which I envisaged would not have been sufficiently 'professional' to count towards this sea time.

I am sad that it does not seem possible to implement such an idea because the length of time a young man or woman can remain in one position with one organization is limited to about two and a half years minimum and probably four years maximum. After that the responsibility for the ship and enabling the crew to gain the most of their time on board so drains the skipper, mate or bosun, that they either have to leave or they withdraw into a sort of protective shell

Malcolm Miller's stand by part of the duty watch.

Brigadier Robin Duchesne
with his exchange crew
from seven different
countries.

and become much less good at the job. If you take the case of a 25-year-old who has skippered a 70 ft sail training ketch for three years and has become mentally exhausted, what is he going to do next? Work in an office? Sell insurance? There are not many jobs now available with the same degree of responsibility coupled with outdoor adventure and a high degree of job satisfaction.

At last we come to those young people, the crew. In previous chapters I have tried to describe what I believe the young people can get out of their time on board. Here I would like to look into the make-up of the ideal crew. I believe the most important factor is that they should be as mixed a bunch as possible. In many years of sail training I have so far only had three impossible crews, with whom I could do nothing; two of them left the yacht before the end of the voyage and the third I shipped home early. They had learnt nothing and had left me in a state of great anger and unhappiness because I felt that I had failed them. They had failed to react to any of the aspects of sail training and I was left profoundly depressed. In each of the three cases, they all came from a common source, the first was a scout troop, the second a public school class and the third a community home (approved school as it was formerly called). Middle class scouts, upper middle class public school pupils and working class delinquents, all from quite different social classes but in each case, they knew each other extremely well before they joined and the sail training magic failed to work. Of course this is not an instant and irrevocable recipe for disaster, and I have sailed with many excellent crews drawn from one source. However, there is always an extra element of risk that if they do all know each other before they join the ship and if they do not know the ship's officers, then an 'us against them' situation may arise.

Equally, I feel that even if the crew members do not know each other before they join, there is a potential problem if they all come from the same environment or the same job. With a complete crew of police cadets, of soldiers, of nurses, of public schoolboys, of borstal boys there is always a chance of it not working. Certainly those ships which regularly take whole crews of youngsters in trouble, criminals, drug addicts and so on, have a nearly impossible job. The wear and tear on the captain and his adults is enormous and there have been several cases of ports refusing entry to such ships after the crews have run amok on a number of occasions. I should add that I am talking about the medium and small sizes of sail training craft; in the big ships, it is inevitable that the crew will come from the same organization, the navy school, the merchant navy academy etc, but as they are part of a disciplined organization undergoing a formal period of training, the same problems do not arise.

Let us look at two sizes of young crew, firstly the size that one would find in the average 70 to 80-footer, 12 young people and secondly the 40 or so that would be in the 100 to 130-footer, and let us consider the composition of the ideal crew. In the case of the twelve, not more than two should be young people in trouble because other than in very unusual circumstances, two bad apples will probably not be able to turn the whole barrel rotten. Of course they will try, the normal pattern being that, without consciously realizing what they are doing they will attempt for up to two days to swing the system around to their own way but due to the strength of character of their leaders at various levels, they fail. The third day is spent sulking because they have failed, and then on day four and five they very often become the best two in the crew. This is because usually they have great strength of character and personality and they appreciate any reasonable antidote to boredom and, curiously, are immensely loyal to anyone or any system that earns their respect. That is probably the main reason they were in trouble in the first place. Two delinquents then, and if possible not more than two.

Of the remaining ten, any combination of social levels and employments will work, the wider the scope the better. If I had to choose an ideal crew of twelve with which to work, I might take two delinquents, two public schoolboys, two comprehensive schoolboys, two apprentices from industry, two police cadets and two youngsters who were unemployed but not in trouble. All boys — and in pairs why?

Let's deal with the pairs first, since it's the least controversial. Having warned against large sections of a crew being drawn from one

At least there is a chance to relax sometimes.

source, nevertheless I recommend strongly that youngsters are not sent on their own. It is quite a shock to most of them to find themselves in the totally strange environment of a boat or ship and it is always reassuring for them to know at least one other person when suddenly plunged into these strange and bewildering surroundings. Not more than two though, because we start to have a problem if too many of the crew know each other before joining with a potential 'us' against 'them' situation.

Yes, but why all boys? I have strong theories about this with which many of you will not agree; what a pity that it is not possible to discuss this through the medium of the written page! I believe that in the case of sail training yachts up to 80 ft, the voyage crew should be either all male or all female. If you have both sexes, there is a strong and natural tendency for the girls to step back from the rough, tough and horrid jobs while the boys push themselves forward with a tendency to show off, sometimes with dangerous results. The whole business of learning to live on board, to master the basic skills necessary to sail the boat are going to demand a great deal of concentration from the youngsters and that concentration may tend to be broken by the presence and the challenge of having the opposite sex to vie with. Of course it can work and has done in many different sail training organizations. I know of one very successful voyage where the crew of 18, 12 boys and six girls, was

divided into two watches of boys and one of girls. No concessions
were allowed to the girls; if a square-sail had to be clewed up and
stowed when it was their watch — up they went and got on with it
extremely successfully. The Ocean Youth Club takes any combination
of boys and girls as a matter of course and that, too, works extremely
well. However, if I was planning the ideal crew for the normal length
of time of one or two weeks that the youngsters are on board, then I
would make it either all boy or all girl.

Now to the crew of 40. Basically I believe the same rules apply as
for the crew of 12. In this case three delinquents can be supported,
but even with this larger total number any more than three can be a
disaster. Otherwise as wide a mixture as possible is the ideal. I
believe that it is also important to draw up the watches with some
care. When I have to do the job I make sure that anyone from the
same school, job, even town is put into a different watch (although if
there are more than three I have a problem). Once the crew of 40
has been divided into its watches, it is not very much different to the
crew on board the smaller ship. Of course, it takes longer for
everyone to settle down when in groups of, say, 13 rather than of six
but with good watch leaders and encouraging watch officers, the
mixture is very much as before.

So, I have tried to describe the ideal crew although, like the ideal
vessel, there isn't one. What never ceases to surprise me is how crews

Sedov's two huge wheels.

This picture captures something of what the Sail Training Association tries to do by organizing their races.

can have an identity. Of course individuals can, it would be an impossible world if this was not the case, but a crew, a group, how can it have individuality? You begin to sense it on about the third day and the good points can be accentuated and encouraged and the bad ones damped down. The weather helps a great deal although not always in the most obvious way. Those long, hot sunny summer days with the off-duty watches lapping up the sun, with the ship hove-to and a boat launched so that hands can swim, with gentle breezes allowing full sail to be set and the ship ghosting through the water are great, but these are not the voyages that are remembered; rather the spring and autumn passages, with sudden squalls meaning a very quick reaction to get sail off her as soon as possible, or a long, cold beat to windward with the relief of finally making port, and a mug of hot soup once the ship is snugged down and before turning in. It is the hard voyages that engender the stories long afterwards:

'Hey, do you remember that time when all the masthead electrics went out because we'd been hit by lightning?'

If you talk to a youngster who has done an easy summer passage and then to one who has had heavy weather and a tough voyage, you will almost certainly find that the latter has got more out of the time spent on board.

From time to time we have the opportunity to try to choose a crew for a special event. This may be a selection from a number of youngsters who have sailed with a scheme in the previous two seasons and having done well been asked to put themselves forward for a race crew, or a special delivery crew, and if the selection is successfully carried out then the results may well be that of the nearly perfect crew. I believe that for such a selection what should be done is to put them all through a series of tests similar to those employed by the armed services in the selection of their future leaders. Suppose 100 candidates apply for a position in the crew from which you are looking for two crews each of 12 youngsters. Then I am sure that it would be wrong to total up their grades on each of the tests and merely take the 24 best; that will not get you a good crew nor will it be in the young candidates' best interests. Take the top four or five because you will need them when life becomes difficult, but too many high-achievers will get on your nerves and the nerves of each other. Having decided how many you should take from the top of the pile and then probably rejected all those at the very bottom, the selectors should then concentrate on the great mass in the middle of the achievement order. Each should be carefully discussed. Is there a strong need to go? Has he or she got any special abilities, such as playing a musical instrument, speaking the language of one of the countries to be visited, is he a brilliant cook and so on. Is he or she a natural comedian or a clown (you can only really give space to one of each in a crew)? It is these middle men and women who will form the backbone of your ideal crew.

The ideal crew must be the one that you would really like to sail with again. One that when it is time to sign them off, you feel as if between you you could pick the ship up and carry it bodily if required. That is the ideal crew, and it only happens very occasionally.

The Holy Ground

(I understand that the Holy Ground is the name of a Pub in Ireland).

CHORUS

And we'll sail the South Sea over,
And then return once mo-r-e,
And still I live in hopes to see,
The Holy Ground once more.

FINE GIRL YOU ARE!

Fare you well, my Din-a-h,
A thousand times adieu,
For we're going away from the Holy Ground
And the girls we all love true,

And now the storm is rag-i-ng,
And we are far from shore,
And the poor old ship is tossing about
And the rigging is all torn,
But the secret of me heart, me dear,
You're the girl I do ad-o-re,
And still I live in hopes to see,
The Holy Ground once more.

And now the storm is ov-e-r,
And we are safe and w-e-ll,
And we'll go into a public house
And we'll sit and drink like hell.
We'll drink strong ale and porter
And make the rafters r-o-ar,
And when our money is all spent,
We'll go to sea once more.

Chapter 8
Finance and Safety

Finance and safety may seem an unusual combination of subjects for the same chapter, but my excuse for banding them together is because the second is a quite large proportion of the first! Because so much of the world is to one degree or another in an era where inflation is quite considerable and an unknown quantity from year to year, it would be misleading of me to quote actual figures. What may be a reasonable figure as this book is published may not make much sense to a reader in, say, four years time. I am therefore concentrating in most examples on guide-lines rather than quoting actual figures.

I find it an interesting fact that quite a large number of different organizations which have started sail training schemes in various countries and largely independently of each other, have after careful consideration come to very similar conclusions in a number of areas and their financial structure is one of these. In Chapter 6 while discussing the ideal vessel, I concentrated on three sizes of vessel, the 70 ft yacht, the 140 ship and the sailing ship of over 250 ft. The reason for selecting those three sizes is that they are the three most common chosen by many organizations after they have tried to define the most financially viable size of craft. Two of the most important financial criteria upon which the budget is likely to be based must surely be the number of crew that can be carried and the length of voyage for which they will be on board. This gives rise to a very simple calculation of the income that can be raised from voyage fees, and what is more this source is the most tangible. Experience has shown that the 70 ft yacht usually sails with 12 novice crew supported by 7 or 8 people whose experience has been tried and tested; the 140 footer normally has 40 youngsters supported by about 15 with experience, and the large ships take between 200 and 300 cadets with, say, 80 permanent crew, but remember that in this case the crew are on board for perhaps three months rather than one or two weeks. There is another procedure which is used by a number of organizations in slightly different ways, and that is to take a complete crew of adults on certain voyages and arrange their time on board in a similar manner to that for the more usual crew of young trainees, or to adapt the voyage so that it is more of a holiday cruise, but with the temporary adult crew doing most of the work. The Dutch sail training association which operates *Eendracht* employs this method, moving its schooner down to warmer latitudes in the winter, and charging adults considerably more to sail in the ship than they do the young crews in their home waters during the spring and summer. In New Zealand they do the same thing in a slightly different way. They operate a series of ten-day voyages for the young sail training crews followed by a long weekend cruise for adults — who pay relatively more for the privilege. They have found that these adults are quite happy to be treated in a similar way to that of young trainees, provided that the voyage length is not too long. This is well-illustrated by a conversation between a captain of the *Sir Winston Churchill* who walked across the bridge to his starboard lookout, who happened to be a board member of a very large and well-known company.

'Are you enjoying your time on board, Mr Smith?' he enquired.
'Oh yes, it's wonderful,' he replied.
'Don't you mind a humdrum job like being a lookout?' asked the Captain.
'Certainly not, it's marvellous. I'm only responsible for gazing out from the bow around to the stern and even if I do see something, all I have to do is to tell him,' pointing to the officer of the watch. 'Mind you,' he added, 'I wouldn't like to do it for more than six days.'

Another principal source of income is that of a fund, often called a bursary fund, which is topped up by donations from charities, sponsors, patrons or other sources.

Returning to the matter of voyage fees, my advice to anyone contemplating the formation of a sail training scheme would be to set their target for fund-raising not merely to achieve the purchase price of the ship or yacht, but to aim for a considerably larger sum. The income can then be used to subsidize the young crew members for whom the scheme is being founded, for they almost certainly will not be able to afford to sail if they have to pay the full amount of what it costs the organization to take them away. There are many parallels. Take, for example, the campaigning of a twelve metre for the *America*'s Cup — and here I will quote figures because they are comparative. I have heard it said that the yacht costs a mere £450,000 or so to build and equip, but the total budget needed to mount a reasonable challenge is in excess of £5 million. Perhaps a similar situation is the stately home that you are contemplating giving to the National Trust. Sadly they will not accept it unless there is also £2,000,000 or so with which to endow it and pay for its maintenance. In the case of the sail training ship, the buildng is just one hurdle and the daily cost of running it will be just as formidable a problem.

To use comparative figures again, in 1986 the cost to an

organization to take a young person away on a 70 ft sail training yacht for six days was probably about £250. The majority of the youngsters who would benefit most from the experience of being on board almost certainly would not be able to afford the voyage fee, and neither could their parents. What is more it would be a most depressing figure for the youngster to contemplate having to try to raise himself, and equally such a fee would certainly preclude him from sailing again the following year, should he be chosen as a future leader in the scheme. Virtually all the organizations realize that some degree of subsidy is needed or they just will not be able to find enough youngsters able to sail with them. The degree of subsidy is arguable; some say that 25 per cent should be found to assist the youngsters, others say as much as 50 per cent. This balance has to be raised by the organization providing the training. In most European countries, government and local government are unwilling or unable to assist very much, if at all. There was a time, in the 1960s when in Britain, at any rate, they would subsidize youngsters up to half their voyage fees but that was one of the things to suffer in official cut backs. In some countries such help is still available, for example in New Zealand their two schooners *Spirit of Adventure* and *Spirit of New Zealand* are very much helped by the education authority and time spent on board is taken out of the school terms.

Well then, how can these subsidies be obtained or how can a bursary fund be established and kept topped up? The answer is 'with difficulty'. In previous chapters I have touched upon four possible sources. The first was sponsorship, and there is no doubt that commercial companies spend a considerable amount of money in advertising, which is usually the fund from which sponsorship monies are voted. However, you seldom get something for nothing in the financial world, and if a sail training scheme is to be granted sponsorship then the company expects some return, and in the ordinary course of events this is difficult to supply. If the ship is to enter a race or rally, particularly if it carries the name of the sponsoring company, then a great deal of publicity and interest can be generated; the company may be able to entertain some of its influential customers on board, meet the crew and feel part of the event. This is also possible other than in a gathering of ships but with perhaps less of an impact. The organization might agree to taking some of the company's employees at a reduced fee, and in fact there are several schemes which can be worked out between a sponsor and the operator of a ship whereby the former feels that an adequate return is available. Patronage is somewhat similar to sponsorship but without the commercial connotations. Sadly, however, there are very few people around who can afford to be generous to the extent of providing and subsidizing a sail training craft. What a pity that sail training cannot provide something of the excitement of twelve metre racing.

There is a very great deal of money available in the hundreds of charities which have been set up over the years and in many cases the trustees of those charities find it quite difficult to find causes that come within their deeds of gift to whom they can make grants. If the mythical sail training scheme which we are setting up can come within such parameters then here may be a most useful source of funding. The type of youngster or the area they come from might provide the right trigger here.

Finally, 'other sources'. These might be companies and individuals who sponsor one berth per year or who give commodities such as fuel or food items free of charge or groups of people who join together for operations such as fêtes, coffee mornings, raffles and many others. There are all sorts of well established methods of earning income and a few rare and successful ones that people will keep very much under their hats!

Where is all this money going? Having built and equipped the vessel it still has to be run and maintained. Nowadays in virtually every organization the biggest drain on funds is the wages bill. In the case of the 70 footer, if the ship is to have a permanent captain then he will have to be paid, presumably a wage on which he can live. It may be decided that he needs a second permanent person on board, possibly a bosun who may well be a youngster under training and therefore commanding a relatively small wage or, more expensively, it may be a mate who will need a wage nearly similar to the captain's but with the bonus that he may be able to stand in for the captain when he goes on leave or in the case of sickness. It may also be decided that some shore organization is required, to process the applications for berths, organize the refits, food deliveries and so on. This might be done by a paid organizer and it might even be necessary for him to have a part- or full-time secretary. On the other hand any or all of the above might be volunteers (you will remember the case of the London Sailing Project where all the sea-going appointments were filled by volunteers), but the snag is that such a system creates considerably more wear and tear, if not damage, to the yachts which then costs money and time to put right. The project has a part-time organizer, a part-time secretary and three full-time staff to look after their three large yachts and associated boats and land transport.

A newly-formed organization will have to evaluate carefully how many staff are needed and how much can be done by volunteer labour, usually an extremely keen source of help but one that often needs a great deal of professional guidance. In the case of the two larger sizes of ship, the 140 footer and the large sailing ship, then the possibility of using unpaid people and even the decision as to the number of ship's staff that are to be employed will almost certainly be taken out of the hands of the organization as it will be dictated by the appropriate maritime authorities. These larger ships will be of such a size as to be treated as classified ships and will therefore be subject to the many and various regulations regarding their country's rules on

manning, safety equipment and so on. Furthermore the ships' staff will probably be professionals and will therefore be entitled to laid down periods of leave so consideration will have to be given to hiring people to stand in for them during this time, otherwise the ship will have to be taken out of operation for lengths of time sufficient to allow for this leave.

There is another alternative which is to find suitably qualified volunteers to stand in for the permanent officers, perhaps without pay or at a reduced wage, because there is no doubt that as well as being a highly responsible job and a demanding one, for a professional mariner to take a 'busman's holiday' in a large sailing ship is not without a great deal of enjoyment. As an example, the Sail Training Association which operates the two 140 ft schooners *Sir Winston Churchill* and *Malcolm Miller* each of which has a captain, chief officer, engineer, bosun and chef, employs three captains, chief officers and engineers and has a source of suitably qualified stand-ins for the bosuns and chefs. That, as you can imagine, means that they face a hefty wage bill to which have to be added the wages of the shore staff.

Food is another large item of expenditure. Unless the young ladies and gentlemen are very seasick, the fact that they are in the open sea air and working hard at heaving up the sails and so on will make them eat even more heartily than usual and who has not watched with astonishment the capacity of a seventeen or eighteen-year-old to

A new cadet signs on aboard the Swedish Navy schooner *Falken*.

Right and below Crew from a number of different ships report on board *Sedov* at the start of the Crew Interchange.

dispatch food? Happily I cannot think of any sail training scheme that has tried to economize on food; it is an extremely false economy and would very quickly lead to that organization getting a bad name amongst its followers.

Despite the fact that this is a sailing ship, it will still need a considerable quantity of fuel both for the auxiliary engine and in addition, possibly for both a generator and for cooking. However much the shore organization instructs the captain to economize on fuel, there are often times when either the arrival at the final port would not be achieved on time with the consequent delay of disembarking the old crew and embarking the new one or, in mid voyage, periods of calm which would possibly ruin the impact of the voyage if they meant that the ship either had to stay in harbour for extra time or was just 'a painted ship on a painted ocean', with nothing for the youngsters to do for hour after hour. At least by motoring, the ship is going somewhere and some sense of purpose is engendered. Any captain worth his salt will want to sail at all possible opportunities and will plan his passages to take advantage of the wind's direction, but in the summer months there are often long periods of calm.

Of course the sails themselves cost a great deal of money and they have a limited life, particularly when handled all the time by novice crews. One must not forget that these are working ships rather than pleasure craft. It is probably fair to say that the average privately-owned yacht is in commission from April to October and may be used, say, every other weekend throughout that period together with a two or three week summer holiday; the sail training yacht probably starts its season in March and stops at the end of October, sailing week in and week out except perhaps, for three periods of one week when it is in port for maintenance. Its working sails, therefore are likely to last for only three seasons. A mainsail for a 70 ft yacht cost £2,000 in 1986! The same 70-footer probably sets in addition to the main, a mizzen, a fore staysail and a working jib; the mizzen staysail and genoas are probably used less frequently than the working sails and so will last for, perhaps, five seasons rather than three.

I am leaving all safety equipment for the moment, so apart from that, food, fuel and sails are probably the three most expensive items of ships' costs. However, there are many more items which need maintenance or replacement. Amongst these are ropes and items of specialized clothing such as oilskins which because they are so specialized are unlikely to be owned or available to the youngsters. The sail training organizations invariably supply them to the crew while they are on board. There are also harbour dues and berthing fees, pilotage fees, charts and navigational publications, the list is seemingly endless.

Then there is the winter refit! Whatever size of ship is envisaged, each will have to be maintained to a high standard and proof will be needed by the maritime authorities that this is indeed being done. In

Repairing sails of this size is tough work.

the case of the yachts, most organizations have a survey carried out by a qualified surveyor at least once every four years and as a result various recommendations will be made on the survey report. It would be foolish and potentially dangerous to ignore such advice, so work will have to be put in hand. Some of it almost certainly beyond the skill of the scheme's own personnel and required to be done by a boat yard or shipyard, and therefore incurring more cost. I will risk a figure again and say that the average annual yard bill for a 70 ft wooden yacht built before the war in 1986 was about £20,000 and for a fibre glass yacht of the same size built in the early '80s was £10,000. It is also likely that as the boats get older so they will cost more to refit. But, and it is a big but, those figures are only averages ones. Should the yacht need a new engine, re-decking, major work done to planks or frames, then the figures I have quoted become unrealistic. Furthermore they are yard costs which will include large amounts of labour charges, and they are extra to the work carried out throughout the winter by the permanent crew and by any working parties of youngsters who have sailed with the scheme, always provided that the yard allows such work to be carried out on their premises. If they do allow this, a good working party of youngsters can save a great deal of money if they are properly supervised and if they are given labour intensive jobs but without too much skill attached. By that I mean, for example, preparation of the outside of the hull for painting and then the application of the various coats of paint or the preparation and varnishing of deck houses, hatches and so on, and cleaning and painting down below including the dreaded bilges. My experience is that ordinary young crew are far from ideal as a source for working parties as they do not have the motivation and lack the concentration to carry out this kind of work for the length of time required. If possible the level of watch leader should be used, that is youngsters who have sailed in a previous season and have been singled out to sail again as a young leader. I also strongly suggest that at least some of the permanent employees of the scheme are present all the time that work is going on and that rather than becoming involved in jobs themselves, they disassociate themselves from practical work and are thus able to exercise overall supervision, re-task the youngsters when required and ensure that the necessary stores are available and not wasted.

Young people and paint can be a lethal mixture. I remember vividly an occasion when I came on deck to find a young crewman sploshing about in a 14 ft wooden lifeboat, secured in its chocks high up on the deck of the *Captain Scott*.

'What's going on?' I asked.

'Oh 'eck, oh 'eck' came a wail from the boat. 'T' bosun'll murder me!'

From the hysterical bystanders I pieced together that the luckless

A delicate piece of engineering.

Scrubbing ship can be fun.

lad had kicked over a 5 litre container of International Dayglow Orange paint inside the boat, had sploshed sadly round trying to scoop it up and then acted on the advice of an accomplice who'd suggested:

'Pull out the bung and I'll hold a spare tin underneath.'

He had, but the wind had then caught the paint and diverted it away from the empty tin and splattered it all over the inside of the bulwarks which the bosun and his dayworkers had recently repainted. The bosun had just finished describing the lad's lack of parentage and general lack of affinity with things nautical when I had happened by. We invented a new ship's rule there and then which was never to give paint in quantities of more than one gill at a time to any trainee — like all young animals the answer was little and often!

Incidentally the same lad was often in trouble throughout his time on board. On another occasion he was posted as bow lookout, right up in the eyes of the ship — the deck of which was some 120 ft long:

'There's a buoy, a fishing buoy,' he shouted aft to the bridge.
'Where abouts?' bellowed the officer of the watch, peering worriedly forward and realizing the consequences of getting gear wound into the propellers. The lad was running back to the bridge.
'There, there,' he puffed, as he ran back, pointing over the side.

He and the buoy arrived in the area of the propellers at about the same time. Still, I am happy to be able to say that despite the paint, the buoy and several other nautical disasters, his keenness and enthusiasm for everything that he had done during his time on board was rewarded by his being presented with the ship's ensign that had flown during his voyage, the prize that was awarded to the member of the crew seen to have made the biggest improvement whilst on board.

However, boy and girl labour is not all bad. Mistakes are bound to be made, but with skilled supervision labour charges can be reduced and the youngsters made to feel proud of the efforts that they have put into the maintenance of the boats which they enjoy sailing during the season. The permanent crew's ability to carry out jobs will inevitably vary according to their training and ability. In the best cases they can carry out repairs and alterations to the accommodation, engine overhauls and so on. It should be remembered though that in the case of the 140 footers and larger, as I have pointed out, they will come under the jurisdiction of the maritime authorities and a lot of this technical work will have to be carried out by qualified fitters and shipwrights.

I can summarize the sources of annual income and expenditure of an organization running two medium-sized ships, in this case the *Sir Winston Churchill* and *Malcolm Miller* by quoting the following approximate percentages:

INCOME		EXPENDITURE	
Income from voyage fees	66%	Sea staff salaries	30%
Income from donations	24%	Stores and maintenance	19%
Investment income	8%	Headquarters expenses	16%
Miscellaneous income	2%	Food	12%
		Fund-raising expenses	5%
		Fuel	4%
		Insurance	3%
		Miscellaneous expenses	11%

One very important fact that many of the existing organizations has discovered is that to run one boat, whether it be a 40, 70 or 140 footer, is not an economic proposition. The work load on the shore organization certainly does not double with the second vessel, but the income from its voyage fees does. If a complete system is set up for one ship it will work very well for more than one with a consequent saving of staff and therefore of wages. Having said that I do believe that in the case of sail training organizations, small is beautiful. I do not recommend too large an organization because then it becomes impersonal and those who take part tend to lose their individuality.

I would like to turn now to the subject of safety and the expenses and highly specialized equipment which are needed to minimize any danger to which this training might expose the young crews. I mentioned in the first chapter that this is adventurous training and that therefore there is an inevitable element of danger linked to it which adds the spice and is undoubtedly an important ingredient. I said that this danger can be minimized by establishing a set of rules and ensuring that those rules are kept. It is a well-known fact that such rules and all procedures and practices of seamanship will vary from organization to organization, hence the well-known nautical saying, 'Different ships, different long-splices.'

In many cases there is more than one way to tackle a problem or an evolution and often different crews get very parochial about their drills. That is all very well provided that the drills carried out and the equipment provided on board are commensurate with good seamanship and safety. Unfortunately it is all too easy to decide quite categorically that such and such is a waste of money and it is not therefore available on board. It is frightening to hear a skipper with a great deal of sailing experience say that he does not believe in flares, and I have heard such a statement more than once, or:

'We don't believe in life-rafts, too expensive and anyway we've got a dinghy.'

The problem is that safety equipment is extremely costly, only lasts for a limited time and is expensive to maintain and replace. In addition everyone is quite certain that it will never happen to them and they will never have to use the wretched things anyway. There are many publications available recommending the scales of equipment for different sizes of vessel and we who are taking novices to sea should make every effort to ensure that should anything go wrong, either they will be safe or the problem can be put right.

There are recommendations with regard to life-rafts for small craft and mandatory rules for the larger ones. If any vessel, be it a sail training yacht or a sailing ship, is going outside sheltered waters, by which I mean harbours, rivers and canals, it must comply with them. Of course, they are hideously expensive to buy and also to maintain, needing an annual inspection and overhaul with consequent renewal of their certificate or, if this is witheld, the purchase of a new life-raft, and because they are a sealed unit which is re-packed by the servicing agent no one can argue against their recommendations. They just have to pay up or replace according to advice. However, it is an expensive fact that if they have to be used they save lives and it is criminal to try to get away from carrying them on board in a properly-maintained condition.

It is difficult to believe but during checks of safety equipment before a long offshore race, the officials concerned will find all sorts of horrors; for example, some boats without a life-jacket for each person on board or life-jackets that were bought second-hand shortly after the War and now have rotten fittings or torn coverings. Some owners seem not to believe in the value of safety harnesses for their crew. It is another well-proven fact that properly-constructed harnesses with the correct type of hook and of adequate construction will keep a man in the boat rather than allow him to fall into the sea. I suppose, like the seat-belts in motor cars, it can be argued that on certain rare occasions they can cause more problems than if they were not fitted but statistics have proved that in the majority of cases when they are needed, they save lives and minimize damage. One life-jacket and one safety harness per person on board, or a garment combining the two, must be the rule.

Fire extinguishers are another potential source of worry. Like flares and so many other items of safety equipment, they do not last for ever, they need maintaining and, according to the manufacturer's recommendations, replacing from time to time. If you look carefully around people's boats I believe you may still find the odd ex-War Department pump-type extinguisher, operated by a pump action and filled with carbon tetrachloride. I am advised that this chemical will put out the fire, and is quite likely to put out the crew as well, due to the subsequent generation of toxic chemicals.

Now to flares. I spent some years as a flare demonstrator for the Royal Yachting Association. After we had demonstrated and fired some of the latest flares, we used to invite the yachtsmen, who had been previously advised of the facility, to fire off any of their own flares so that they could get some practice and experience of what it felt like when one was ignited. The recommendation was to fire off some of their recently time expired ones, but often the word 'recent' was widely interpreted because some of the items produced, with chemicals oozing from them, were quite terrifying. I would not have touched them, let alone contemplated firing them.

I have mentioned the provision of oilskins or foul weather gear. I believe that it is essential that a sail training boat should carry sufficient equipment to clothe the whole crew against foul weather. This is specialized equipment and anyone to whom a sailing voyage is other than a regular experience will not have adequate gear and to sail in heavy weather without it is not merely just miserable, it can be downright dangerous, with the risk of those not adequately clad experiencing hypothermia. Ideally some pairs of sea-boots should be available as well. In the mid-1950s when more knowledge became available about hypothermia and its effect upon people exposed to cold for long periods, many yachtsmen realized that the crew member slumped in the open cockpit who had lost all interest in his surroundings and who feared to go below at the end of his watch because of seasickness, may well have been in the first stages of hypothermia. Nowadays experienced yachtsmen are aware of the problem and therefore take precautions for their crews.

I hope now that you have read the preceding few paragraphs you are shaking your head and asking yourself why I bothered to write such obvious facts. The reason is that we have found so many otherwise competent and sensible people who refused to acknowledge the need to provide many of the items I have mentioned.

On the matter of safety drills, I believe these, too, are of the greatest importance. Every single person on board should be required to put on their life-jacket and safety harness with a watch leader or someone of experience supervising and assisting if necessary. Before the ship gets underway, there should be a briefing on 'man overboard' procedures, the launching and use of the life-raft and any other drills and signals that may be employed on board. What is more, these drills should be practised from time to time during the voyage. In a few cases 'man overboard' drill is religiously practised during the first few hours of sailing and then never thought of again. A woolly sailing hat blown overboard, a piece of timber in the sea or any similar opportunity can be taken to carry out another drill at some later stage during the voyage. I find that I spend quite a lot of time thinking out various actions that I might take should someone fall overboard, the ship catch fire or any other disaster occur. I do not believe that this makes me a scaremonger, but that it establishes certain thought patterns in my brain, so that should any of these disasters occur I will have already been through any action which may need to be taken once or twice before in my mind. Of one thing I am certain: however flexible and efficient a drill, each incident will have associated with it its own individual problems and these may well call for a non-standard reaction.

As an example, we were anchored in Village Bay on the island of St Kilda, outside the Outer Hebrides when one of the boys fell overboard. In an instant two other lads jumped over the side and swam to his assistance, supporting him and attempting to bring him back to the ship against the tide. As quickly as possible we launched a boat and got the victim and his two rescuers into it and eventually back on board. So? So the last thing that is normally done is for anyone else to go over the side thus adding to the number of people who needed to be rescued. However, in this particular case, although totally wrong, those two boys may well have saved the third one's life.

Incidentally while on the subject of 'man overboard', a topic that must have engendered more argument and discussion than almost any other connected with sailing, the immediate reaction of a crew going to its stations, throwing markers to the victim, pointing to him continuously and the getting of the vessel back to where he is in the water and stopped close to him are two possibly routine matters. It is getting him back on board that is often dismissed as a final and easy problem hardly worth discussing, but it may well be the most difficult part of the rescue and one that needs a great deal of thought. It may well be that a life-raft is the main solution for it would give some kind of platform to support the victim should resuscitation be necessary and while preparations are made for getting him back on board. I can think of more than one fatality that might not have occurred had someone thought to put some kind of boat or raft into the water as quickly as possible.

Perhaps I can end this chapter by telling a story against myself which mixes up boats and safety. It is against me, but does help to emphasize the care which is taken to look after the young crews, particularly in small boats in a fairly open stretch of water, a time when they are at greater risk than when on board a sea-going yacht. The occasion was the work up before a transatlantic race and we had

Far right More teamwork — this time on a haliard.

Right Standing on a Flemish Horse at the yardarm.

Far right That's a nice stow on the staysail.

Below The STA Mobile Office and tug.

Right 'To enable young people from many nations . . .'

Below Prize Givings are always exciting occasions for the young crews.

put into Cherbourg during a practice sail. For various reasons the skipper had anchored off in the inner harbour and so, when there was an opportunity for shore leave, the crew had to be transported by dinghy. Now we had a Coypu, a small general-purpose boat which can be rowed, sailed or propelled by outboard motor. On this occasion it had been decided to get the crew ashore under sail. Each group donned life-jackets and one of the watch officers took charge of the boat and off they went, until it got towards the end of the number and the only person left to take charge was a young man from the sailmaker who had sailed with us to check out several new sails.

'Can you handle a sailing dinghy?' I asked him.
'Yes I think so,' he replied solemnly.
'Right, then just let me see you sail her round the yacht,' I told him and he dutifully jumped in and, single-handed, sailed the dinghy very competently round.

Satisfied, I allowed the last shore-goers to get into the boat and off they went. As they sailed away from the yacht's side, the skipper popped his head out of the deckhouse:

'You obviously didn't realize that Ken is an Olympic dinghy helmsman,' he said.

Salvation Band

by Roger Watson

(Sung in a broad Yorkshire accent!)

CHORUS
S-a-l-vation Band with their big trombone
And the music fair goes through you,
With their Onward Christian Soldiers! and their Glory Hallelujah!

When I was just a little lad on Sunday morning early,
Salvation band came down our street to make their hurly-burly,
Well, they all stood round in a great big ring and started blowing cornets
An' all the kids from miles around came swarming up like hornets.

There were scores and scores and scores of kids, perhaps there were even thirty,
And goodness knows who owned them all but they all looked filthy dirty,
There was Jackson's kid from across the street an' 'e were a right young villain,
When t'collection box came round to 'im, 'e made off with fifteen shillin'.

Now the man as stood up and waved t'big stick looked tall as 'alf the 'ouses.
'E'd got a brand new uniform with gold braid down the trousers,
Be'ind 'im stood little Tommy Jones wi' 'is young grey pup called Dusty,
Now the pup must'a thowt t'man were a tree 'cos gold braid's gone all rusty!

Now t'rest reckoned band wer'n't up to much, but me, I didn't mind 'em,
So when they upped and marched away I marched along be'ind 'em.
We marched to t'other side of town in streets I'd never been in,
And finished in t'yard of a public 'ouse as me Dad said I shouldn't be seen in.

Now when the policemen fetched me 'ome, they'd had their dinner without me,
When me feyther found out where I'd been I knew for a fact 'e'd clout me,
Well I got t'buckle end of me Dad's pit strap and that were plenty for me,
I've never followed that band again and that's the end of me story.

Chapter 9

The Tall Ships Races

I will be shot for calling this chapter the 'Tall Ships Races'. As I write they are the 'Cutty Sark Tall Ships Races' and the reason is that they have been sponsored by Cutty Sark Scotch Whisky since 1972. I am a firm believer in sponsorship because I consider that without such support a great number of worthwhile activities, both sporting and otherwise, would not be able to take place. You should have realized by now that I believe very strongly in the enormous amount of good that can be done for young people by taking them offshore in sailing ships and the races are, in my opinion, the epitome of sail training. I therefore deem them to come into the category of a worthwhile activity.

Until about 75 years ago a great number of artistic and some sporting endeavours were patronized by rich people who believed in the achievement of the artist, sportsman or whoever was being patronized. Sadly in the present day very few people are in a position to patronize anyone, and activities that would otherwise be patronized now stop or turn to some other source of funds, perhaps from commercial companies. In that case, for the very reason that they are commercial and because they have to answer to their boards of directors and to their shareholders, they are entitled to some return for their munificence in the form of acknowledgement of their support and, provided the acknowledgement does not detract from the dignity of the event being sponsored, then both sponsor and sponsored should be happy. So, please accept that every time I write the words 'the races' I do in fact mean the Cutty Sark Tall Ships Races.

The reason for including a chapter on the races is because, as I have suggested, I believe that they form a high point in the programme of various sail training organizations throughout the world. In many cases, the cadets or trainees whose time on board just happens to coincide with a race are particularly fortunate because, having talked to many youngsters in that situation, there is no doubt that they have gained considerably more out of their particular voyage than others who have merely done a routine voyage which did not

Royalist showing how handy
a brig can be.

include a race. In other cases where crews are chosen with great care out of quite a large number of applicants, and once chosen become the crew for the race, their progress within their particular scheme is almost certainly going to be enhanced. They will stand a better chance of becoming a future watch leader and eventually watch officer, and moreover probably become amongst the best of their scheme's leaders.

The words the Tall Ships Races conjure up an exciting kaleidoscope of impressions, of giant square riggers with towering masts and billowing sails leaning majestically to the wind, of sleek schooners sliding gracefully through the water. Proud young people wearing different uniforms, from many different countries, work together to extract the last ounce of efficiency from their vessels and do their best to win their class in the race. Later the ships are alongside some jetty, a multitude of flags fluttering in the breeze, the bustle of maintenance and preparation for the next voyage.

Like so many things, it all started in a small way, with the dream of a retired London solicitor named Bernard Morgan, a dream of a brotherhood of the sea. Why not bring together the youth of the

world's seafaring people in friendly rivalry and at the same time
further their learning of their profession and of themselves? As so
often happens when someone has an idea, Bernard Morgan started to
talk to anyone who was interested and probably to quite a few who
were not! One of the people to whom he talked and who listened
was Commander Peter Godwin and by 1954 the two of them had
put together a proposition which the Commander placed before Earl
Mountbatten, who was at that time the First Sea Lord. He liked the
idea and sought the expert opinion of Captain Illingworth, one of the
world's experts on offshore racing.

In the autumn of 1954 John Illingworth formed a committee which
they called the Sail Training International Race Committee (STIRC)
to organize what was to be the first Tall Ships Race to take the
entries from Torbay to Lisbon in July 1956. One member of that
committee who worked tirelessly towards the success of the first race
was the then Portuguese Ambassador at the Court of St James,
Senhor Pedro Theotonio Pereira. The committee also received a
great deal of support and assistance from the Royal Navy, particularly

Eagle is a Coast Guard
cutter as well as a sail
trainer.

Creole — is she somewhat like *Sir Winston Churchill*?

from Britannia Royal Naval College at Dartmouth and from Admiral Munn and Admiral Crawford. Mr Ray Barratt was also immensely helpful and evolved a system of measurement and handicapping for this first race which survived in one form or another until 1968. In Lisbon one of the key organizers was engineer Luis Lobato who could clearly see the good effect that the race was having on the young crews. He was subsequently to be involved as the chief organizer when the fleet returned to Lisbon in 1964 and again in 1982. As we shall see, he was also to form the Portuguese sail training scheme, Aporvela, as a result of the effect which he saw achieved by STA over the years.

This first race was an outstanding success, so much so that the committee decided to make the STIRC a permanent body in order to keep the expertise together and to organize future races every second year at the suggestion of the operators of the square riggers.

This newly-formed committee approached the Duke of Edinburgh, who paid them the enormous compliment of agreeing to become Patron, an office he has held to this day. Bernard Morgan's dream had not only become reality but the scope had been exceeded as there was now a permanent committee whose aim was to make the reality recur. In June 1956 Articles of Association for the Sail Training Association were signed and the STA as I shall now call it, came into being.

The first Chairman of the Council of STA was Captain John Illingworth whose experience as an ocean racing skipper was of inestimable value in the planning of the races over this early period. Hugh Goodson was Chairman of the Sailing Committee and Bernard Morgan Secretary. In 1958 a race was run from Brest to La Corunna, with 12 entries and concurrently another from Brest to Las Palmas, with 17 entries including three square riggers.

John Illingworth remained as chairman until the end of 1962 and the STA continued to flourish, organizing a small race in 1960 with five entries from Cannes to Naples, and another, a much better supported event, from Oslo to Ostend with six square riggers (three of these from Norway) and 12 smaller entrants. Sadly Bernard Morgan had to resign as Secretary in December 1960 due to ill health but he kept a close interest in the STA until his death. Another man who put an enormous amount of work into these early races was Commander W. J. P. Church who in 1958 was Assistant Director of Naval Training. On retirement from the Navy in March

Ah well! That's another Start safely over.

1961 he became the Secretary of STA when Bernard Morgan retired. It was a great shock to STA when Commander Church was killed in a motor accident in April 1963. The report for that year says 'During the years in which he was our secretary he had worked tirelessly on all aspects of sail training including the appeal for our own sail training vessel'.

The 1962 race, with two square riggers and 27 others, saw the beginnings of a larger fleet. It was an exciting and windy race starting from Torbay, racing round a mark-ship off Ushant and thence to the finish off Rotterdam. It is interesting to imagine the effect such a course would have today on the dense volume of shipping ploughing up the Channel, through the Dover Straits and so to the Europort; such a plan would be quite out of the question.

At the end of 1962, Captain Illingworth handed over the Chairmanship of STA to Hugh Goodson who had been a keen supporter of its work since the Association's inception. He was keen both in administrative support and also helping financially because the small amount of money that was needed in those days was found by the committee, mostly I believe from their own pockets. STA owes a great deal to all of them for establishing the foundations upon which later committees and officers of the Association have built.

The first series of races of the Goodson dynasty was a challenging and complex one in 1964, starting from Plymouth and racing to Lisbon, thence, after an enjoyable stay, to start off Cascais and race across the Atlantic to Bermuda. Fifteen vessels raced down to Lisbon where they joined the square riggers and eight of these (again three from Norway) were joined by four relatively small yachts for the transatlantic leg to Bermuda, one of which was *Tawau* whose participation I mentioned in Chapter 2. Thereafter the fleet cruised in company to New York. This was the first race to be under the direction of Colonel Dick Scholfield. Dick was another keen ocean racing skipper, well known to John Illingworth who had asked him to retire early from the army and take on the job of organizing the Tall Ships Races. He brought his experience as a racing man and a long-standing committee member of the Royal Ocean Racing Club to the problem of running the Tall Ships Races. He introduced a classification of the fleet with the square riggers forming Class A and the smaller fore and aft rigged vessels split into two divisions of Class B. Dick started work, with the advice and help of yacht designer Colin Mudie, to produce an STA Rule of Rating which set out to try and give an even chance of success in a race for every competitor, be they 3,000 ton barques or 20 ton ocean racers. This rule was used for the first time in 1968.

The whole 1964 race series was a great success, but gave rise to considerable dissatisfaction that Britain, which organized the races, had no tall ship of her own. However, this brought to a head the work which Hugh Goodson had been doing to remedy this. He had been working very hard to try to achieve a sail training ship for

Britain and had established a Schooner Project Committee under the chairmanship firstly of Maldwin Drummond and then of David James. He also started a fund-raising campaign to pay for the ship once the decision had been taken to go ahead and build and this was chaired by Lord St Aldwyn. The driving force behind this determined effort to build a large training vessel for Britain was that of Hugh Goodson, ably assisted by James Myatt and his navigator in the 1964 races, Commander David Cobb, both of whom bent to the task of assisting in the efforts of the STA plans to have a training ship built.

The keel of a Charles Nicholson designed 300 ton topsail schooner was laid in 1965. The original hull design had been commissioned by the Southampton School of Navigation and Captain Wally Wakeford, a very keen supporter of the STA and a member of its council, allowed the design to be used. With a rig designed by John Illingworth the *Sir Winston Churchill* was built by Richard Dunston at Hessle near Hull, and launched there in February 1966. Shortly after she started to operate, through the generosity of the then Lord Mayor of London and ex-Lord Provost of Edinburgh, Sir John Miller, the STA was able to order a sister ship, *Malcolm Miller*, named as a memorial to his late son. She was built by John Lewis of Aberdeen and launched in October 1967. These two schooners have had many critics, both as to the layout of their hulls and of their rig; however, no ship can please all its critics as I have tried to point out in Chapter 6. Suffice it to say that the ships are still going strong over 20 years later and they have given a great opportunity to a very large number of young people.

In 1965 the first minor race was run from Southsea to Cherbourg with only seven entries. However, 1966 saw a better field when six Class A ships and 24 others raced from Falmouth to the Skaw and thence to Copenhagen for the Royal Danish Yacht Club's centenary celebrations. A small 'get you home' race was organized from the Skaw to Den Helder and another Southsea to Cherbourg race saw a fleet of six Class B vessels.

In 1967 there were two more Southsea to Cherbourg races each with seven entries. Then in 1968 came a double race with a fleet of three Class A and six Class B vessels starting from Gothenburg and racing to Kristiansand via Fair Isle, to be joined there by a fleet of 21 Class Bs racing up the North Sea from Harwich. In 1969 there was a Southsea to Cherbourg race again with 13 entries and a race from Weymouth to St Malo with 11 entries.

The 1970 races consisted of a double race with simultaneous starts from Plymouth with four Class A plus 13 Bs racing to Tenerife and 19 Class Bs racing to La Corunna. In the same year 13 Class B vessels raced from Southsea to Cherbourg and six from Weymouth to St Malo. These latter courses were repeated in 1971 with seven and six entries respectively.

By the end of 1970 Lord Burnham had taken over the Chairmanship of the Sailing Committee with the Hon Greville Howard as his Overseas Vice-Chairman and Brian Stewart the Chairman of the Schooner Committee, but otherwise the hierarchy was largely the same as it had been in 1967. Also in 1971 a race was organized in the Mediterranean where it was believed that there would be great interest because of the increasing number of large sailing vessels operating in those waters. Sadly this did not prove to be the case and the race was great fun but not well supported.

In 1972 another increase in the size of the fleets was experienced with a very successful race from the Solent to the Skaw followed by a cruise in company from Malmo to Travemunde. During the cruise an idea which had been tried in a very small way in 1964 was expanded — that of a crew interchange. James Myatt organized a change round of several of the young crews of the race entrants in such a way as to mix the nationalities and the type of vessel. Thus a British boy from a 70 ft yacht changed to a Swedish 120 ft schooner and so on. This was a great success and was to become a very popular feature in future races. It will not at first be appreciated what an enormous amount of work is involved to ensure that such interchanges are carried out in a sufficiently responsible a way as to calm the anxieties of captains who are sending their young crew members to sea in other vessels. A great deal of careful planning is undertaken to ensure, for instance, that a 16-year-old goes to a ship where there will

Barclay Warburton III, founder of the American Sail Training Association with Greville Howard, 'Father' of the STA Races and Engineer Luis Lobato, founder of the Portuguese Sail Training Association (*Aporvela*).

be others of his age and not a crew composed of 24 and 25-year-olds, or that a young girl goes to a boat where there are already other girls. Everything has to be meticulously logged, which on one occasion paid dividends.

Black Pearl and *Royalist* — two similar sized brigs.

The incident occurred in 1979 when a one-day fun race was organized while the fleet was at Port St Mary in the Isle of Man. Brigadier John Codner organized an STA crew interchange for the race. Unfortunately a gale sprang up out of nowhere and by late afternoon the fleet was scattered into seven different ports. John recruited a fleet of local buses and cars and with his excellent system was able to get every single interchangee back to their own ship with the exception of one young lady who was enjoying herself so much where she was that she would not go back to where she ought to be! The main race consisted of three Class As and as many as 38 Class Bs, 16 of the latter going home via a race from Heligoland to Dover.

One of the entries in the 1972 race was the small brigantine *Black Pearl* owned by Barclay Warburton who had sailed her from the United States specifically to take part in the Tall Ships Races. As soon as they met him the STA race committee recognized that here was a man who understood absolutely the aims and ideals of the races. He thoroughly enjoyed the series and was easily persuaded to think about the possibility of starting a similar association in America. This he did and paid STA the compliment of borrowing its aims and organization and incorporating them into the American Sail Training Association, which in 1978 was affiliated to STA. Since that time ASTA has arranged yearly races in North and South American waters and transatlantic races in 1980 and 1982 to join the American fleet to the European Races, although since the loss of *Marques* in 1984 and the distressing amount of compensation claimed, they have had to restrict role somewhat. Similar associations are being started in Australia and New Zealand.

The races had so far always been administered by a salaried staff of just two people, a director and his secretary, although for a short while between 1973 and 1976 there was an assistant race director. This very small team is augmented by members of the sailing committee and other dedicated supporters who give up their summer holidays to form a race committee and go to the various ports to administer the fleet. In nearly all cases they are sailing folk themselves and many of them act as skippers and mates in the various sail training schemes operating throughout the year. They work exceptionally hard and without their enthusiasm (and they have earned the admiration and respect of both the organizers in the various ports which the races have visited and of the competitors), the success of the races could never have been achieved.

Over the years a number of specialized roles have emerged, the crew interchange being one whose work I have just touched on. The communications team embarked in the communications ship also have a complex task and their patient control of the radio schedules has earned them a great deal of praise from the fleet. There is also a team which carries out checks of a sample of the entrants' safety equipment to make sure that they are complying with our rules in this respect. Then there is the marketing team which does yeoman work manning a stall and selling souvenirs whose sales help to cover the race budget. This also indirectly maintains a good contact with the crews and discovers many of their feelings about the races.

In 1973 a new minor race was started after an idea of James Myatt's. This was a Clyde race which after a certain amount of 'whipping in' produced a fleet of 12 class Bs. Five Bs in one Southsea to Cherbourg race and six in another meant a quieter year, ready for the major year in 1974. Now the team splits and simultaneous starts from Copenhagen and Dartmouth took fleets to Gdynia and La Corunna respectively; 19 Class Bs in the latter and six Class As and 23 Class Bs in the main race. From La Corunna, 22 Class Bs raced back to Portsmouth where they were joined by some of the Baltic fleet. Then followed a cruise in company with a crew interchange, which included a parade of sail in the Solent (producing some spectacular photographs including one of *Kruzenshtern* sailing past HMY *Britannia*), followed by a passage to St Malo and finally a 'get you home' race for those who were going that way, back to the Nab Tower at the entrance to the Solent. This was the first year that the USSR ships had been entered and with the Polish vessels who

entered in 1972 widened the international aspect of the races
considerably. It was also the first race in which a new schooner from
Holland, *Eendracht*, took part. She has subsequently entered nearly
every race which STA has organized since that year.

Although 1975 was a minor race year, it was quite a busy one.
There was a great gathering of sailing vessels at Amsterdam where, in
addition to the sail training fleet, there was a large number of
traditional Dutch barges belonging to members of their flat-bottomed
boat society, also steam tugs, motorized ducks, an animated maritime
Heineken barrel — all imaginable forms of aquatic vehicles. At the
end of the Amsterdam festivities a small race was organized to Den
Helder and from there to the Thames where the newly formed
Association of Sea Training Organizations, a national body to

represent British Sail Training Schemes, had organized a Festival of Sail based in the Pool of London and the newly-opened St Katherine's Yacht Haven.

Throughout 1975 plans were forging ahead for a very elaborate series of races to be run in 1976 to culminate in the arrival of the sail training fleet in New York, where the ships would join with a large fleet of naval vessels and provide a spectacular item in the USA's bicentennial celebrations. The series started with a race from Plymouth on 2 May, which took the fleet to Tenerife in the Canaries. Whilst in Tenerife a short cruise in company was arranged so that, with the youngsters changed over in the now well established crew interchange, the fleet sailed down the coast of Tenerife island to spend the night in the little fishing port of Los Christianos. This particular event is etched forever in the minds of the organizers for, on catching sight of the first square rigger rounding the headland of the port, the harbourmaster, chief pilot and mayor ran away, not to be seen again for the rest of the visit. Some quick thinking by the STA team enabled James Myatt to become the pilot and arrange for the class A ships to be anchored, John Hamilton assumed the mantle of the harbour master and berthed the Class B vessels and John Codner elected himself as mayor and arranged for a party to be organized on shore for some 800 people — and that very much cuts a long story short!

From Tenerife the fleet sailed across a windless Atlantic to arrive in Bermuda in mid-June and, after a memorable stay, a third race started for Newport, Rhode Island. This start was horrific in that it involved two collisions, each between two of the giant square riggers. Much film has been analysed and many are the theories as to why they happened but although extremely unfortunate, happily they had no lasting repercussions, and although one young sailor was badly injured there was heartfelt thanks that there was no large loss of life — which could easily have been the case.

Despite this tragedy the fleet arrived in good order in Newport where they were received and entertained in a most amazingly hospitable manner. Now the key date in everyone's mind was 4 July 1976 — Independence Day, the day on which the most impressive sail training fleet ever mustered to date was to sail up the Hudson River, under George Washington Bridge, wheel round and sail down again. The plan for Class A ships, whose air draft was too high to negotiate bridges on Long Island Sound, was to sail south of Long Island, while Class B vessels sailed through the sound, stopping off at various harbours where numerous clubs had arranged to entertain the crews of groups of vessels — and that was some entertainment, I can vouch for it.

The parade was even more successful than had been envisaged and the whole Tall Ships programme was reckoned by many Americans to have been the most ostanding item in their year of celebrations which, incidentally, changed overnight the whole ambience of the races; from being relatively small affairs with the fleet getting on with its own entertainment, they became massive spectacles drawing literally millions of visitors to most of the ports at which the ships called. The 1976 programme ended with a 'get you home' race from Boston to Plymouth to get the European ships back across the Atlantic and to give the fourth crews a race, because many ships had changed crews several times along the route thanks to a series of charter flights organized by the STA.

So ended 1976, a classic year and another milestone in the development of the races, also the swan-song of Colonel Dick Scholfield who retired in August that year, to be replaced by his assistant — myself. Dick Scholfield had been race director from 1963 to 1976 and had supervised the growth of the Tall Ships Races, had instituted many ideas and established the name of STA as being an organization which runs enjoyable events but in a responsible and fair manner. Perhaps this attitude, which many competitors have found in the races, can be summed up by an American skipper who, some months after trying hard to get the rule about trainees' ages waived so that he could sail with a 15-year-old on board said:

'Well I got to realize that the Colonel wasn't going to give, so it wasn't any use going out and lobbying the crowd, he just wasn't going to change his mind . . . that saved me three days' work!'

Dick's period as race director created a rock-solid foundation upon which has been built the increasingly elaborate events attracting even larger fleets and embracing more and more nations. At the time of his retirement, the office which had been previously located in his house, was moved to Gosport the large town on the opposite side of the harbour from Portsmouth; one of the main reasons for this location being the fact that some seven British sail training organizations have their headquarters in the area. I established this new office with a great deal of help from Jo Brigham, who worked as my secretary from 1976 until 1980 and her enthusiasm was infectious, both in the setting up of the office and when we were away in the ports organizing the races. When she left, Jennie Lennard took her place. She took to the job like a duck to water and rapidly became as deeply involved as so many others to whom sail training is not so much a job as a way of life. Jennie has done a great deal to enhance the 'family' aspect of these events by her warm personality and her ability to transform the dullest letter or instruction into a personal missive. Another important figure in the world of sail training appeared during the 1976 races, the mate of the Dutch naval ketch *Urania*, Bernard Heppener. In 1977 he took over as her skipper and remained so for most of the rest of his service until he retired in 1984. However, in 1976 at Boston, for the return race to Plymouth he asked if he could help the race officials at the start, which he did. His close involvement and interest in the races led to his becoming the first chairman of the Netherlands Sail Training Association, STAN, when it was subsequently founded in 1984 as well as becoming STA's national representative in his country.

The Queen's Silver Jubilee marked 1977 and one of the highlights of that year's programme was Her Majesty's review of her fleet. STA organized a race from the Solent to Le Havre and the novel aspect of this was that the race fleet did not rendezvous in a port prior to the start but proceeded from their home waters directly to an anchorage area on the edge of the naval fleet from where, after the review, they proceeded to a starting area outside the Solent and so raced to Le Havre. It all worked, with the necessary papers such as sailing instructions and communications schedules being delivered individually by launch, and they had a good race. That year saw the last of the Clyde races, because the interest in the event had fallen off. The fleet now consisted almost entirely of the Clyde racing yachts entered

'Your Majesty. May I have permission to carry out the normal starting procedure of the Sail Training Association?'

by some very good and very competitive yachtsmen who, due to their very competitive nature, found it impossible to surrender the helm and other vital jobs on board to a bunch of enthusiastic if unskilled youngsters. So the race was beginning to lose its aim as a sail training event geared specifically for ordinary young people.

Perhaps 1978 was a routine year, with the race organization notable for having been started and finished by Kings. HM The King of Sweden did us the honour of starting the race at Gothenburg amidst a most amazing number of spectator craft and HM The King of Norway presented the prizes in the Oslo City Hall and reviewed the fleet as it sailed from the port. One rather nice touch at the prize-giving came at its end. During a previous visit to the Palace, the chairman of the race committee, Greville Howard had said that it was STA's usual custom to call three cheers for His Majesty at the conclusion of the presentation.

'On no, you cannot do it,' he was told, 'it is against protocol.'

Greville did not argue, which was surprising. However, at the end of the ceremony he stepped forward and said:

'Now at this point I would normally ask you to give three cheers for His Majesty the King, but I've been told not to. However! The King is an Admiral in the Royal Navy — THREE CHEERS FOR THE ADMIRAL!'

The assembled youngsters, some eight hundred of them, nearly lifted the roof of the city hall — and the King smiled graciously.

1979 was another minor year with a Class B race to celebrate the millennium of the Manx Parliament which was very much enjoyed by those who took part. HM The King of Norway who had been invited by the island for the celebrations asked if his visit might be timed to coincide with the race and he graciously agreed to present the prizes again. This time at the end of the ceremony he said:

'I understand that it is the custom to call for three cheers at the end of your prize-givings.'

The King himself then led the crews in three cheers for their hosts, the Isle of Man organizers

The year 1980 was quite an ambitious year with a gathering of the fleet at Kiel. It would have been irresponsible to start a race from the fiord or its approaches due to the restricted waters and the dense amount of shipping and the shipping lanes. Thus the fleet had to leave Kiel and proceed independently some 80 miles to an achorage near Gedser. Inevitably there was a gale during their passage to the area, but despite this all vessels managed to arrive at the anchorage, cope with fishing nets laid from the shore for a distance of a mile seawards and a 24-hour delay to allow the wind to abate and then to start in good order for a race around Gotland to end at Karlskrona.

Much use of VHF radio was made to maintain control of the fleet

'Two young crew members on watch.'

and some quite heavy weather. However, it was a challenge and, in retrospect, enjoyed by the participants. The arrangements at Southampton were extremely well done, the fleet support team worked well under the organization of Captain Chris Phelan and the activities for captains, officers and crew left them breathless — but happy. Princess Alexandra presented the prizes in one of the most family-like occasions anyone could remember.

Although 1983 was supposed to be a minor race year, it appeared that the division between major and minor years had all but been eliminated. The only difference now is that the majority of the larger Class A vessels do not normally take part in the odd-numbered years, although the Class A Division II ships, such as *Royalist, Soren Larsen* and *Asgard* do wish to compete.

In June, STA was asked to 'umpire' the Bremerhaven Hochsee Race and Brigadier Robin Duchesne and I went to the Weser where a small but enthusiastic fleet raced into the shoal waters at the mouth of the Weser and Elbe, and in the area of Heligoland. *Sedov* the USSR Fisheries Board four-master, and the largest sailing vessel in commission in the world, came to Bremerhaven for the event. She manoeuvred in the river off the town for the Parade of Sail where she looked remarkably spectacular in the river, but was not able to take part in the race because the course was in very restricted waters.

In July 1983 STA organized a Cutty Sark Tall Ships Race in the Baltic, mustering at Travemunde where, after a well-organized programme, the ships paraded out of the Trave to a starting area off Gedser, similar to that used in 1980. Then they sailed the same course as that year, round Gotland and so to Karlskrona. This small Swedish Naval Port again excelled itself with a programme every bit as good as that of 1980 and with the King of Sweden presenting the prizes in the town square.

So to August with another Cutty Sark Tall Ships Race, this time in the English Channel. Starting at Weymouth — again an excellent programme and arrangements — the race went around Eddystone for all the fleet except Class C Division II who were sent around Wolf Rock, to end at St Malo where the yacht club responded magnificently, but the town less so.

It was in 1983 that it became obvious that the team of only two permanent employees, Jennie Lennard and myself, was no longer adequate to organize these events which were continuously growing in size and scope. Specifically it is was no longer feasible to merely lock up the office in early July and return again once the races were over, in August, which had been the practice over the years. Consequently Janet Bradbury was engaged, at first on a part-time basis and, in 1986, as a full-time secretary. She, too, has cultivated a great interest in the whole business of sail training.

In 1984 there was an extremely comprehensive series of races

Sedov heading into the wind during a parade of sail.

which celebrated the voyages of Jacques Cartier in 1534. A fleet gathered at St Malo for a race which was started at the Eddystone Lighthouse, took a compulsory stop over of 72 hours in Las Palmas, then went on to Bermuda where an American fleet joined, having raced up from Puerto Rico.

The combined fleet raced from Bermuda to Halifax and it was on this leg that some of the fleet encountered winds of exceptional and unpredicted force. *Marques* was hit by a local squall and sank in less than two minutes with the loss of 19 lives, 9 people being saved by the Polish entry *Zawisza Czarny* and the co-ordination of the escort frigate *Assinaboine* of the Canadian Navy. This tragedy, the first fatal one in the history of the races, cast a great sadness over competitors and organizers as well as over the public. STA's sympathy went out and still does go out to the families and friends of those who were lost. The series continued with a cruise from Halifax to Gaspé and on up the St Lawrence River to Quebec where many of the crews changed and where a mammoth series of events was organized for the fleet and the tens of thousands of spectators.

After Quebec the fleet sailed back down the St Lawrence Seaway to Sydney (Nova Scotia) to start a return race across the Atlantic which ended on Merseyside. In addition there was a European Race from Frederikshavn in Denmark around the North Coast of Scotland which finished at Greenock on the Clyde. Here another crew interchange was organized and the fleet sailed south to Merseyside where they managed to arrive on precisely the right day to meet those who had been doing the Atlantic circuit. STA's limited staff could not have coped with such a long and ambitious programme without some careful deployment. The usual teams covered St Malo and Bermuda then Frederikshavn, Greenock and Merseyside while a team led by Captain Chris Phelan advised the American Sail Training Association in Canada for Halifax, Gaspé, Quebec and Sydney. The radio schedules for these races were conducted from late April until early August by the small team of Jennie Lennard and myself, during which the communications vessel would pass the daily positions of all the ships in the fleet and we would calculate and pass back to them the theoretical corrected positions of the ships within the race. A comprehensive reporting system was established with Janet Bradbury's assistance, both at Gosport and, later, from wherever we were organizing the European race, so that parents and friends of the crews at sea could know of their fortunes. The skipper of the maxi racer *Canada Maritime*, ex *Great Britain II* entered in the double transatlantic marathon was a 25-year-old named Paul Bishop, of whom more later.

The year 1985 was a minor year but this word had by now become rather inappropriate. The ports concerned, Chatham, Zeebrugge and Amsterdam, were told to expect 60 to 80 entries but in the event there were 114! The series started with STA umpiring the Bremerhaven Hochsee race as they had in 1983; there was then a

Left *Velsheda* is a restored J-Boat — even at this angle, her 150 ft mast dwarfs those of *Sir Winston Churchill* and *Falken*.

feeder race from Bremerhaven to bring a fleet to join the main race series at Chatham. A good meeting of the ships took place in the now civilianized dockyard. The Duke of Edinburgh spent some hours with the fleet and met crews from many of the entrants. Off they went on a spectacular parade of sail down the Medway to reappear in the mist on the following afternoon off Margate to start a 'yo-yo' sort of a course up and down the western side of the North Sea, designed to keep them clear of shoals and ships. The weather was most unkind, dictating a beat northwards to round Smith's Knoll and then — a beat — south again to Galloper and thence directly across the shipping lanes to Zeebrugge and through the canal to a great welcome from Brugge. After only two days they cruised in company to join some 800 traditional sailing vessels for the third Sail Amsterdam.

If 1985 was a minor year, 1986 certainly proved a major one. The series started off with a rally of some of the fleet at Delfzijl which proved highly successful and was hugely enjoyed by those who took part. The hosts at Delfzijl did splendidly and organized an excellent programme for the crews. This was the first organizational venture of the STA Netherlands which had been formed the previous year during Sail Amsterdam. The Chairman, ex *Urania* skipper and keen supporter of the race family, Bernard Heppener and his team did a most professional job of organization. The ships cruised in company to Newcastle where they combined to make a large fleet of some 80 ships. Newcastle's organization was also excellent, both on the maritime and on the social side. A great many activities were also organized for the crews with the highlight being a short visit by HM The Queen who walked down a line of representatives of the crews of all participating training ships and spoke to virtually every single

At Bremerhaven, in 1986, over a million people watched the parade of sail.

group. Then she boarded *Sir Winston Churchill* where a representative 25 captains were presented. As ever, Her Majesty radiated charm and interest in everything she saw and left a very proud and happy fleet.

The course for the race to Bremerhaven was direct and blessed with following winds for most of the way and as a result the fleet was early. Different ships had different reactions to the visit to this North German port; those that had good liaison officers and who were able to make the most of the programme, thoroughly enjoyed themselves, others were not so lucky and were rather overcome by the general fairground atmosphere. It was a great honour that the Bundespresident himself came to present the prizes and to review the Class A and B ships when they left on the following day. Sadly the Class C ships did not get reviewed by the President or the public. The passage from Bremerhaven to Larvik incorporated a highly successful crew interchange with some 250 young people swapping between ships.

Larvik was a delight, a small and simple port whose inhabitants gave a truly fantastic Norwegian welcome to their visitors. Virtually everyone in the town became involved with the visit in one way or another and nothing was too much trouble for them. An enormous fleet of 120 sailing ships, including *Sedov* and *Kruzenshtern*, the two largest sailing ships in commission in the world, *Dar Mlodziezy*, *Gorch Fock*, *Statsraad Lemkuhl*, *Kaliakra*, a new-comer from Bulgaria and for

Dutch barges, although not part of a race fleet, adding to the spectacular sight.

Above *Christiania* is a
restored sailing rescue ship.

Right HM The King of
Norway at the start of the
1986 race at Larvik.

a short stay, *Christian Radich* on her way home from New York; Thor Heyerdahl was there, both the famous explorer and the ship — they got together for a day's sail. The Mayor had exhorted his citizens to make the young sailors welcome and they exceeded his greatest hopes. To round off a memorable visit, the King of Norway reviewed the Parade of Sail and then was the official starter of the race to Gothenburg. This port had done exactly what we hoped it would and that was to provide a simple and unspoilt venue for the fleet as a contrast to the bustle of the busy and industrial ports of Newcastle, Bremerhaven and Gothenburg.

To reach this last port in the series, the Class A and B ships raced out of the Skagerrak to round an oil-rig in the North Sea and thence to a finishing line off the Skaw. Incidentally, the oil-rig had been warned to expect the invasion, the idea being to give them a shoal-free race in open waters. In the meantime the Class A Division II and all of division Class C raced on a similar course to that used by a well-known and popular race for yachts, the Skaw Race, around a course inside the Skagerrak. Again the fleet finished early and many took the opportunity to sail among the islands of the Swedish archipelago near Gothenburg. Once in port, the local organizers had laid on good facilities for the fleet although it was sad that because of the bridge and the ferry compounds the fleet had to be berthed in three separate groups, something we always abhor because it negates our endeavours to get the young crews from many different nations to meet each other. An excellent prize-giving followed, with Prince Bertil, the King's uncle, officiating. So ended the 1986 series, having been honoured by three Heads of State and a Royal Prince, with 120

Kruzenshtern prior to the start of the 1986 race.

HRH Prince Bertil of Sweden with the happy winners of the Cutty Sark Trophy in Gothenburg in 1986.

entries in one race and with another generation of young people with a collection of memories with which to help their progress in growing up. In the early part of 1987 Jennie Lennard was unable to work through back trouble. John Hamilton and Janet Bradbury continued the work needed to prepare for the races and in June, Paul Bishop, previously mentioned as the skipper of *Canada Maritime* and subsequently an Ocean Youth Club skipper, joined STA as the Race Director's assistant. His arrival meant that the race organization continued at its usual standard.

As the years have rolled by there have been many changes. Maldwin Drummond handed over chairmanship of the Association to Freddie Cartwright in early 1973 and he presided over the Association's affairs until 1976. He handed over to Lt Colonel The Lord Burnham who, until then had been Chairman of the Sailing Committee. Under Freddie Cartwright the Association continued to expand slowly with the two schooners continuing to provide adventure cruises for large numbers of youngsters. During this period and due to the Chairman's efforts, the Friends of the STA was established and the assets might be available as an emergency reserve, a small one but one that would serve to tide over the Association in a short financial disaster, and thus provide some measure of reassurance. Lord Burnham's place as Chairman of the Sailing Committee was taken over by Admiral Sir Rae McKaig at the end of 1976. Between 1971 and 1985 the Sailing Committee had had joint Chairmen, to give them their full titles, Chairman, Sailing (UK) and (Overseas). A system of joint chairmen could be difficult both for the committee they chair and the directorate. However, in this case it worked remarkably well and the Overseas incumbent, Lt Commander The Hon Greville Howard who had served on the

Above *Goteborg* saw a spectacular parade of sail in 1986 to complement an awe-inspiring start in 1978.

Left Greville Howard with the author.

Council of the Association since its inception in 1956 had become a very highly esteemed figure in international sail training. Over the years, due to his hard work, infectious enthusiasm and considerable financial support of the races, he had established a sail training family, a hard core of dedicated supporters of sail training who appreciate that the races and the policy of the Association provide a high point in their calendar.

Sometimes I see a slight look of cynicism cross people's faces when this word 'family' is used in connection with the races. Perhaps I can take one example, a man who came up to me at the London Boat Show in 1971 and asked about the races which he was thinking of entering. Incidentally he had a Freedom-rigged boat which made our Rule of Rating scratch its head a bit. I told him about the spirit which is engendered and I saw that look. He wrote to me after his first race and admitted that he had hardly believed a word of the family feeling but now he was confessing that he had been wrong. He remarked on the friendly way he had been received by captain of square rigger and crewman alike and how he was only sorry that he had found the races so late in his life. He has done virtually every race since and throws a champagne breakfast on his birthday which always manages to occur during the series — and when he is in port. In 1985 Greville Howard had to resign from his chairmanship through ill-health, but the Association was delighted when he agreed to accept the office of Commodore of the Races, in which capacity he was available as a consultant, acted as an elder statesman and continued to use his personality and influence to enhance the family atmosphere of the races.

Over the years several advisory bodies have been established and the International Advisory Meeting has been held yearly in London from 1971. It was formed as a result of various advisory meetings, starting with a meeting of 'Tall Ships' Captains' held at the Criterion Restaurant in Piccadilly. In subsequent years several social events were combined with the meetings and in 1978 work and the social activities were combined into an annual International Sail Training conference during which were held meetings of the International Advisory Meeting, the International Racing Committee which had been formed by Greville Howard after the very successful 1976 races and the International Sailing Committee formed in 1985. This Conference allows those attending the opportunity to meet members of the STA Sailing Committee and to meet each other both formally and, perhaps more importantly, informally whilst staying in the hotel in which the conference is held.

These conferences have proved to be most successful with very many old friends and quite a few new ones attending each year. STA is usually besieged with requests from ports who wished to invite the fleet, and it is encouraging to note how many ports who have hosted the fleet would very much like to do so again in the future. I am convinced this is not merely because of the financial and commercial benefits which such a visit bring; the fact that the invitation is usually issued almost as soon as the fleet has departed and the spirit in which it is issued leads me to think that the ports really do want this event because of the atmosphere generated by the ships and their young crews.

In 1978 the fleet was re-classified, Class A remaining square-riggers, Class B the large schooners and Class C, the sail training yachts.

Of great sadness were the deaths in early 1983 of two people whose vision, enthusiasm and refusal to accept defeat had given STA the life force it needed to achieve its aims: Lt Colonel James Myatt, who had competed in his first race in 1960, to whom this book is dedicated and whose name has appeared in several places; also Barclay Warburton who had taken the STA message back across the Atlantic in 1972. These two are very much missed, but their example lives on to inspire those who continue their work.

In the 1960s Sir Harold Macmillan was telling us that we had never had it so good, then when inflation began to bite in 1978 many realized that he was probably right. Inflation has hurt sail training and until then the STA had relied very strongly on the personal contributions of its officers, and it still does, because without the voluntary support of committee members and other enthusiasts the races could not be organized as they are at present. Over the period of a Tall

Bernard Heppener, first Chairman of the Netherlands Sail Training Association, receives the Cutty Sark Trophy in 1982.

The STA Race Director
takes a busman's holiday on
board *Colin Archer* while a
watchful owner supervises.

Ships Race, the 'permanent crew' of three at Gosport is augmented
by up to 20 volunteers who give up their summer holidays for
nothing more than their travel and accommodation, and who work
harder and for very many more hours than they probably have to in
the normal course of their jobs in order to ensure the success of the
races.

These financial strictures have been considerably softened by the
increasing sponsorship and support of Cutty Sark Scotch Whisky
who not only provide a fee to help defray the cost of organizing the
races, but also set up arrangements for the press and assist with the
marketing activities. They have also contributed in a large way to the
success and perhaps to the peculiarity of the races by providing the
Cutty Sark Trophy; now this is not given for winning or even for
doing well in the races! It is awarded to that vessel which by the vote
of the captain taking part that year has done the most for international co-operation within the fleet. It was first awarded in 1974 when
Kruzenshtern from the USSR was voted the winner; in 1976 it was
won by the Belgian navy ketch *Zenobe Gramme*; in 1978 by *Gladan*,
again a navy ship, this time from Sweden; in 1980 by the famous
Polish full-rigged ship *Dar Pomorza*; in 1982 by the Dutch navy ketch
Urania, in 1984 by the STA's own schooner *Sir Winston Churchill*, and
in 1986 by the Swedish Cruising Club's ketch *Atlantica*.

So the dream is established, the Sail Training Association is an
internationally respected and responsible body organizing a series of
well-supported international events. Two million people came to
Amsterdam to see the fleet in 1980, in the same year five million
descended on Boston for the same reason. Wouldn't Bernard Morgan
have been proud, had he been there?

. . . and that is the message of the tall ships.

A Glasgow Song

Jorrie = marble
Stink = drain
Claespole = Clothes Pole.

Wee Johnny's lost his Jorrie,
Wee Johnny's lost his Jorrie,
Wee Johnny's lost his Jorrie,
Doon by the Brumielaw.

He dropped it doon the stink,

So he went an' got a claespole,

And he rammed it doon the stink,

But the claespole would'na' reach it,

So he went an' he got his dawg,

And he tied et tae the claespole,

But still it would'na' reach it,

So he went and he got some dynamite,
So he went and he got some dynamite,
So he went and he got some dynamite,
And he blew up the Brumielaw.

Wee Johnny's found his Jorrie,
Wee Johnny's found his Jorrie,
Wee Johnny's found his Jorrie,
Doon by the Brumielaw.

Et wis in his bluidy pocket,
Et wis in his bluidy pocket,
Et wis in his bluidy pocket,
It wis'na' lost at all!

Stupid — but catchy!

Appendix Stores List

In 1970, having recently been appointed as the first chief officer of the *Captain Scott* which was being completed in Herd & Mackenzie's yard at Buckie on the Moray Firth, I asked who was going to place the order.

'Oh. Aren't you?' queried the Captain.

So I did and to my chagrin, when we sailed out of Buckie Harbour for the sea trials, it was soon discovered that we had no teaspoons on board.

Curiously enough I have been asked for a similar list on two subsequent occasions and as I believe it can be adapted for a smaller-sized sail training ship, I feel that it might be useful to include it here. For most of the items I have omitted the quantities of each item and the various sizes as they depend both on the size of the vessel to which the list is being referred and also, in some cases, to taste. So here is a shopping list to fit out a 500 ton topsail schooner — and it does include teaspoons!

Bedding

(This will depend upon whether sleeping-bags will be brought or provided, or if duvets are used)
Mattresses
Mattress covers
Pillows and cases
Sheets/liners/covers
Blankets

Bosun's Stores

Spare wire for running rigging
  (lengths of the correct size to replace one of each size of wire running rigging)
Spare rope for running rigging
  (lengths of rope as above)
Spare 15-thread ratline (unless terylene is used for ratlines)
1 spare masthead flag halliard
6 working and 2 spare mooring lines
4 wire mooring lines
4 heaving lines and spares
Cod line
Boat lacing
Marlin
Log line
Seizing wire
Seaming twine
Roping twine
Plastic tape

Terylene thread — 3 sizes
Sail needles
Palms
Beeswax
Punches and dies
Brass eyelets
Marline spikes
Swedish spikes
Fids
Serving mallets and boards
Tape-measures
Spare canvas
Spare sail cloth
White hide
Grease
Spare blocks of the sizes used on
  deck
Snatch blocks
3 Handy-billies
Chain stoppers
Chain cable hooks
Rubber hose
Funnels
Boat-hooks
Fenders
Old tyres for rough fenders
Ratguards
Sledge-hammer with spare shafts
Spare timber (damage control)
Spare winch handles
Spares for winches
Hammers with spare handles
Cold chisels
Bolt croppers
Punches
Crowbars
Podgers
Stillson wrenches
Shifting spanners
End-cutting nippers
Side-cutting nippers
Axes
Spare shackles of sizes in use
Thimbles
Senhouse slips
Spare anchor cable shackles and
  tools
Marker buoys with strops
Spare hanks and slides (if used)
Bosun's chairs
Hand choppers
Gangway net

Pilot ladder
Sounding rods
Buckets (lots!)
Deck mops
Deck scrubbers
Paint scrubbers
Squeegees
Spares for all sailing boats carried
Spares for other ship's boats
Outboard engine spares and tools
Life-jackets plus spares (valves,
  whistles, lights etc)
Safety harnesses plus spares (lines,
  carabiner hooks etc)
Awning and side curtains
Cones and balls
Anchor light
Emergency navigation lights
Paint
Varnish
Thinners
Scrapers
Chipping hammers
Sandpaper
Holystones

Cleaning Material

Soda
Sand
Brasso
Deck/hand scrubbers
Detergent, powder and liquid
Mops and buckets
Dusters and rags
Sweeping brushes
Dustpans and brushes
Wash-leathers
Harpic
Ajax
Toilet rolls
Soap
Lavatory brushes and holders
Waste bins
Various polishes

Crockery

(The numbers depend on the size
  of the ship and therefore the
  number of people on board)

Plates — dinner, soup, side
Bowls — sweet
Cups and saucers
Mugs
Egg-cups
Serving-dishes
Glasses
Jugs
Cruet sets

Cutlery

Knives — large, small
Forks — large, small
Spoons — soup, pudding, tea

Engineer's Stores

These are so specialized that no list
  can be properly comprehensive.

Fire Fighting

As laid down by the maritime
  authorities.

First Aid

As laid down by the maritime
  authorities.

Galley Equipment

Saucepans — 2 pint, 3 pint, 5 pint,
  7 pint
Rolling-pin
Knives — bread 7 in, cook's use,
  carving, paring, utility
Peelers
Meat-forks
Slotted turners
Basting-spoons
Potato mashers
Tin-openers
Food scoops
Cake-tins
Pie plates
Skimmers
Ladles
Large colanders
Conical strainers

Wire sieve
Nylon sieve
Frying-pans
Deep fryers with basket
Baking/roasting-tins
Flat baking-trays
Graters
Kettles
Meat-axe
Egg-brush
Pastry-brush
Cake cooler
Wire whisk
Set of pastry-cutters
Mixing-bowls
Pudding-basins
Chopping-boards
Jugs — assorted sizes, measuring
Scissors
Funnels, various
Mincer
Food-mixer
Air-proof jars
Jelly-moulds
Bacon-slicer
Chipper
Flan-rings
Piping-bags
Tea-towels
Cleaning gear

Navigation Equipment

Radar
Decca equipment
Possibly Satnav equipment
Echo-sounders
Wind strength and direction
  instruments
Compasses — standard, steering,
  boat, hand-bearing

Patent and electronic logs
Hand lead line
Pelorus repeaters
Azimuth mirror
Parallel rulers
Dividers
Compasses (drawing)
Protractors
Charts — folios as required
Associated publications as required
Sextants
Chronometer (or accurate
  wrist-watch)
Station pointer
Almanac
Tables
Stop watch
Magnifying glass
Binoculars (and cheap ones for
  trainees to drop)
Barograph and barometer
Wet, dry and sea thermometers
Weather forecast plotting sheets
Fair and rough log books
Note books
Pencils
Erasers
Flares — as required
Line throwing equipment

Oils & Paints

Red lead
Red oxide
White lead
Metal primer
Anti-fouling
Preservative undercoating
Gloss topcoat
Varnish

Thinners
Paraffin
General-purpose grease
Tallow
Lubricating oil
Oil cans
Blow lamp
Releasing fluid
Paint scrapers
Chipping hammers
Paint brushes
Paint rollers
Sand paper including wet and dry
Grease remover
Paint-stripper
Linseed oil
Paint-sprayer
Masks
Goggles
Funnels
Steel cans
Plastic cans

Signalling Equipment

Aldis lamp
Boat lamp
International code flags
Dressing lines
Ship's call letter flags
Extra 'Q' flag
Courtesy ensigns
Ship's ensigns
Boat's ensigns
Sea/storm ensigns
House flag
Hand-operated fog-horn
Torches with spare batteries and
  bulbs
International code of signals
Appropriate lists of radio signals

Glossary

Aporvela
The Association of Portuguese Sail Training.

ASTA
The American Sail Training Association.

ASTO
A British Association which acts as a spokesman for British sail training schemes.

Auxiliary engine
Nowadays almost all sail training vessels are fitted with engines in order that their tight training schedules can be met.

Bosun
The Under Officer responsible to the Captain, through the Mate, for all upper deck gear; this includes masts, spars, sails, rigging and deck fittings. Also the state of maintenance of the hull.

Box haul
A manoeuvre which starts as a tack and ends as a gybe; used in a square-rigged ship when ground cannot be lost downwind.

Buntline
A rope running from the foot of a square sail to the yard above; used to haul the bunt of the sail upwards when furling.

Chief Officer
The Captain's deputy; also called the Mate, the First Officer or the Executive Officer.

Clewline
A rope running from the bottom corner of a squaresail to the yard above; used in furling the sail.

Day workers
Those members of a ship's company who work all the daylight hours and are excused keeping the night watches.

Department of Trade
In Britain, the government department which controls shipping; the term Board of Trade is possibly more familiar.

Engineer
The Under Officer responsible directly to the Captain for the maintenance and running of all machinery and electrical gear. A large ship would have a Chief Engineer who is an officer of high rank.

Gybe
Make a fore-and-aft sail or boom wear or run before the wind.

Flares
Special pyrotechnics used to advise of distress or emergency situations.

Fore and aft rig
A sailing ship without yards or one where the sails are predominantly set without their use. The distinction is subtle and is explained in detail in Chapter 5.

Halliard
A rope or system of rigging used to haul the head of a sail or a yard up the mast.

Hand
To lower a sail; opposite of set.

Heads
The lavatory; so called from the primitive planks with a row of holes rigged outboard of the bows (or heads of the ship) in the old square riggers.

Leeward
The side of the ship opposite that from which the wind is coming; the 'downhill' side of the ship and the best side from which to be sick!

Life raft
A special rubber raft with canopy and containing specialist

materials; used like a life-boat if the vessel should sink.

Log

a) An instrument to measure distance travelled and hence speed.
b) A document in which all technical and navigational details of the ship's progress and condition are recorded from hour to hour.

Master

Another term for the Captain; he is also called the Skipper in a sail training yacht.

Mate

See Chief Officer.

Purser

The ship's officer responsible for all accounting for monies and stores.

Safety harness

A chest harness with a length of rope and a special hook, worn when aloft, outside the guard-rails etc.

Sheet

A rope attached to the lower aftermost corner of a fore and aft sail, used to control its angle to the wind or on a square sail, attached to the lower corners and pulled down to set the sail.

Skipper

The term used for the Captain in a sail training yacht.

Square rig

A sailing ship having one or more masts fitted with horizontal yards from which rectangular sails are set.

STA

The Sail Training Association, a British organization which arranges races for sail training ships all over the world and acts as consultant for similar events.

STAG

The Sail Training Association of West Germany.

STAN

The Sail Training Association of the Netherlands.

Tack

a) To turn the ship so that the wind comes from one bow to the other; ie, the bows are forced through the eye of the wind.
b) The bottom corner of a sail nearest to the mast or stay upon which it is set.

Trainee

A young man or woman who is on board the ship to learn; may or may not be a future professional seaman. They make up the crew of the ship and without them it cannot sail.

Watch

a) A group of the crew; usually the crew (less the officers) is divided into two, three or four.
b) A period of duty; usually of four or six hours.

Watch Leader

A young man or woman who has usually sailed before who acts like a Leading Hand in the watch; some racing yachts use this term in place of Watch Officer.

Watch Officer

Usually an adult; he or she is in charge of the watch of young people at all times when they are on duty; they are also responsible to the Captain for the running of the deck when the ship is at sea.

Wear

See Gybe.

Windward

The side of the ship from which the wind is coming; if sick from this side you will 'get your own back'!

Yacht

Yachts are used as vessels for sail training but in this case they are working boats rather than pleasure craft.

Yachtmaster

The highest certificate available in Britain for amateur yachtsmen. Higher qualifications are only available to professional mariners.

Index

Gorch Fock